The Road
to
RACQUE and
ROUEN!

41 RACQUE

ROUEN 71

DeMontfort
FineArt

Acknowledgements

The author wishes to thank the following extremely kind and trusting individuals:-

Helen Swaby; Giles Halliwell; Rosamund Hitchcock; Nigel Barden; Laure Godinot, Guillaume De Castelnau and the directors of Louis Jadot; Esme and Sara Johnstone and all at Château de Gours; Katie Jones and the directors of Mont Tauch; Marie Jose and the directors of Taittinger; Christine Brown; Owen Morgan; Nick Boler (for letting me run riot in his Wine Cellar, purely in the interests of research!) And all the wonderful, kind and patient people stretching from North Yorkshire to the Mediterranean coast who have helped inspire either intentionally or otherwise! THANK YOU!

A Message from the Author

Before His Excellency The President of the glorious Republic of France mobilises his secret services in an effort to track me down and string me up by the Tuilleries may I first of all, PLEASE, crave his indulgence ~ If anything between the covers of this book appears stereotypical, predictable or just plain corny then may I please remind his excellency that I sat my French 'o' level four times and endured much pain and humiliation in the process. However, I am prepared to forgive and forget in an effort to encourage closer ties and a furthering of the Entente Cordiale between our two great Nations.

FOR SARAH

— In memory of my dear friend Nick —

La Mairie
Racque
France

Madame Sandré and myself take great delight in wishing you and your
publication much sucess and are so proud that our town features in such a
prominent way in your new book.
All the people bid you well and hope that it will not be too long before
you are amongst us once more. Monsieur Jean from 'Bar Albert'
has asked me to bring to your attention the little matter of an unpaid bar
bill (two bottles of house wine, five beers, a cognac and a broken chair).
As a gesture of good will the honest people of Racque have held a
collection on your behalf and the cognac has duly been paid for.

Cher ami bonne chance!

Louis Sandré

Maire de Racque

Chapter one

"Y a-t-il un itinéraire touristique
pour aller à Beaune ?"

MY Madcap tour of a few favoured
French Vineyards With Mollie and a Map!

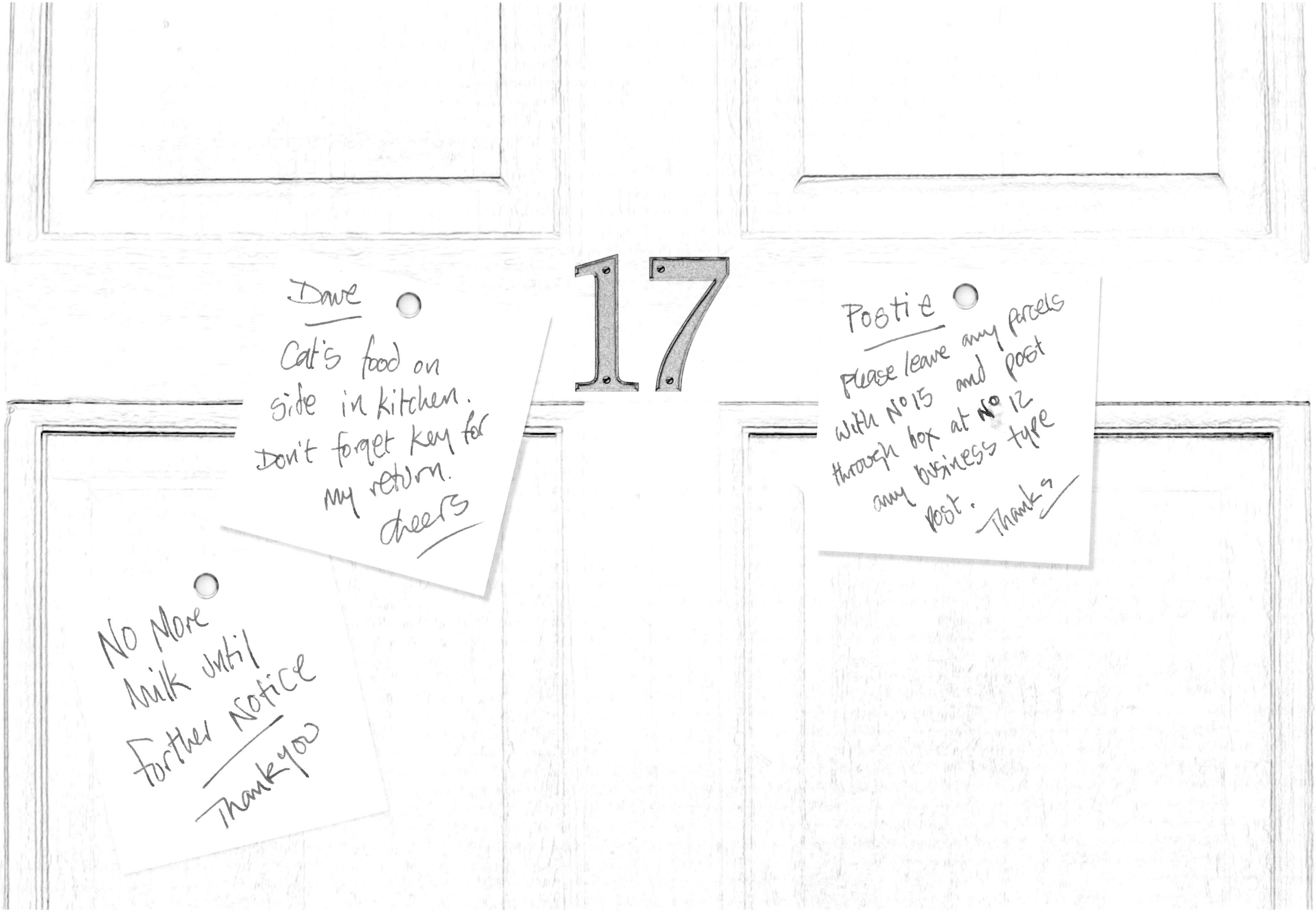

17

Dave

Cat's food on
side in kitchen.
Don't forget key for
my return.
cheers

No More
Milk until
Further Notice
Thankyou

Postie
Please leave any parcels
with No15 and post
through box at No 12
any business type
post.
Thanks

an eye for detail!

A.P.   A Very Private Moment !   TIM

Lunch break!

A few old favourites at
château des Jacques!

An Amusing diversion!

Rush Hour, Tuchan!

A·P.   Salut!   JiM

" Bringing home the bacon ... and the shallots ... some onions .... a little celery .... A case or two of wine ...
the odd loaf ... Aubergines .... A large chunk of Camembert .... cognac ... Garlic ... 36 large snails ....!! etc
etc

A Really stinkingly early start! 3 AM!!

BOOM!

BANG!

like the lost dog in Sputnik!

WAAAA

Meeeow

CRASH!

creep Silently out of Paziols + unnoticed through Tuchon!

I Will Return!

A Massive haul up France from Perpignan to Reims Just look at the Map!!

BACK to Reality!

GAZ GAZ MOTEL

Spend the night in a dull spot but I can sleep uninterrupted for 8 hours! Somewhere in France!

CENTRE VILLE

AEROPORT

PARIS NORD

PARIS SUD

PARIS

IF You don't want to go to PARIS when circling it then be prepared for frustration!

REIMS pronounced Rrrrrr anse

IF IT'S Wednesday IT MUST BE ReiMS!

I eventually Arrive in Reims early in the Afternoon + find the hotel without a hitch. Busloads of American seniors on the French leg of their European tour. A Busy Modern Hotel quite a contrast after the idyllic solitude of Tuchan.

Gee, the last time Elmer+I were here we blew the bridge!

eet eez eezi!

I remember to ask for the directions to Taittinger for the following morning. The receptionist is so darned pretty and animated that I fail to listen to a single word she says!

The Hotel MERCURE REIMS

Aaah! The joys of the Mini bar and CNN News!

HELP!

LINGERIE PARFUMS VINS

The shops come in three categories which conjure up wonderful images of beautifully clad ladies who are all slightly tipsy yet alluringly fragrant.

KER CHING!

ROUGE BLANC

BACK AT The Hotel

Shower and change I have a Real City to Hit!

AH! Maybe NOT!

TRUMP!

DECIDE TO TAKE THE LIFT. It stops for one Nanno second between floors + I naturally keep my cool + remain totally calm!

BUY C.Ds at FNAC Francis cabrel + 'M' and Les Vacances de M. Hulot on video

GO Mad at the Wine Merchant. It's one thing buying the stuff + quite another carting it about!

château Picque callou '97
château Magnan–Figeac '97
château Ferrande Graves blanc
Louis Jadot Pommard la Refene '96

Excellent Supper at REST D'ERLON FAB ESCALOPE de Forestière.

oi MUSH CHIPS!

where's my PINT!

MUNCH! SLOBBER! BIG DAY TO-Morrow!

SADLY WE ARE NOW WITHIN easy reach of the less desirable English elements!

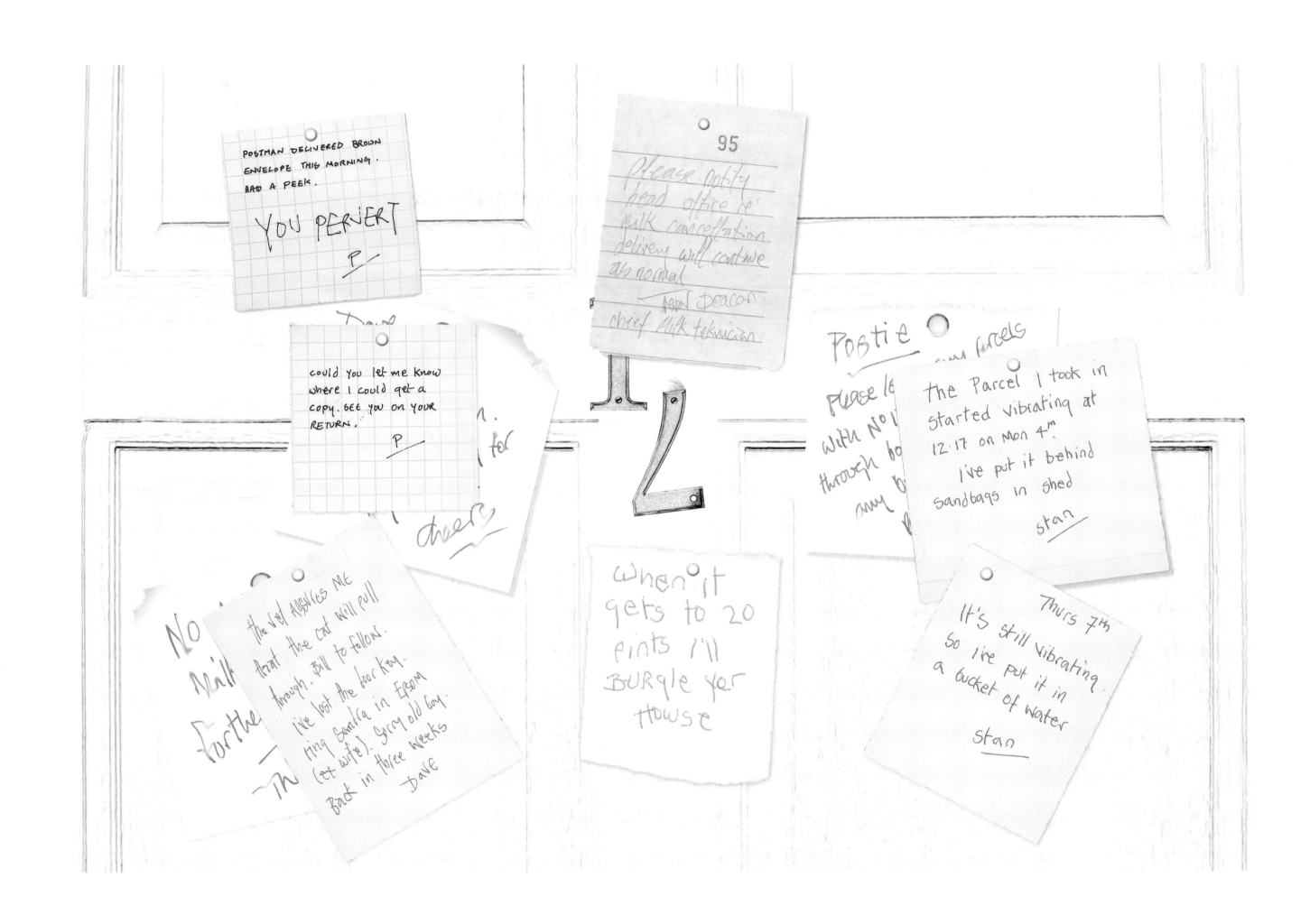

Chapter two
· VIN ·

"Je Voudrais encore une bouteille de Petrus
Pomerol 1975 S'il Vous Plait!"

⧯

When I discover Just how much there is to learn
and sadly how little I actually know!

But Who's Complaining!

Les Vendangeurs!
Happy Go lucky!
Moi j'en ai assez! J'laisse tomber!
Grumble!
There's always one!!
Moan!
Humph!
The Poor Beleaguered Foreman!
Allez! vite!
Imbécile!
Pourquoi?
The Pickers!

The Wine Merchant

The Vineyard Tour Guide!

I have been hugely privileged by being allowed to savour some earth shatteringly fabulous wines with the proviso that I re interpret the labels. Now I don't know about you but I call that a pretty fair exchange!

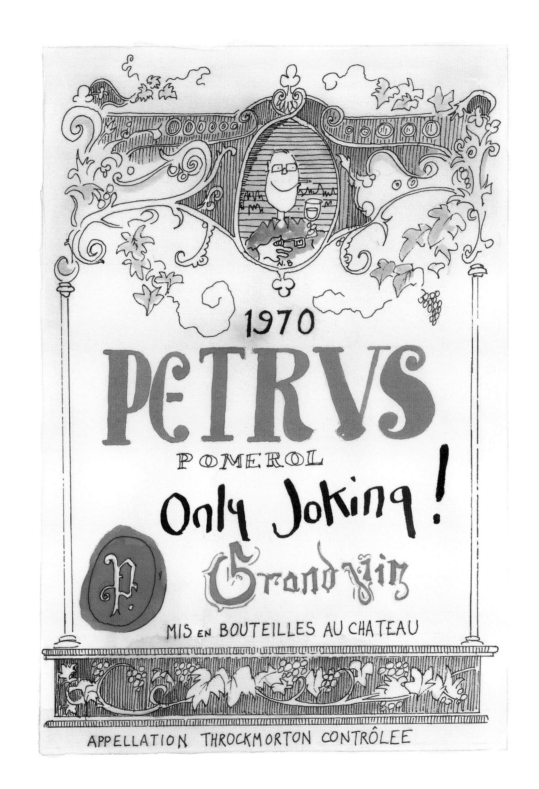

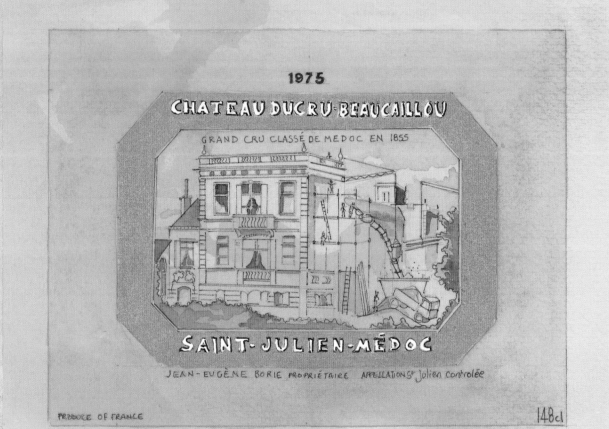

1975

CHATEAU DUCRU-BEAUCAILLOU

GRAND CRU CLASSÉ DE MEDOC EN 1855

SAINT-JULIEN-MÉDOC

JEAN-EUGÈNE BORIE PROPRIÉTAIRE   APPELLATION St Julien controlée

PRODUCE OF FRANCE   148cl

GRAND VIN
DE
CHATEAU LATOUR
PREMIER GRAND CRU CLASSÉ
APPELLATION PAUILLAC CONTRÔLÉE

PAUILLAC-MÉDOC
1962
MIS EN BOUTEILLES AU CHÂTEAU

SOCIÉTÉ CIVILE DU VIGNOBLE DE CHÂTEAU LATOUR
PROPRIÉTAIRE A PAUILLAC-GIRONDE

N. BEAULAIRE & c.
BORDEAUX

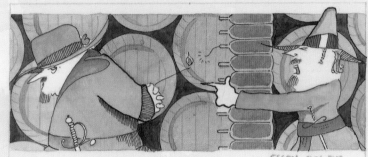

ESSEN BOLEUR

1975

cette récolte   à produit
241.000 bouteilles bordelaises et demies
9.245 magnums, jéroboams, impériales

Philippe de Rothschild

Chateau
Mouton Rothschild
LE BARON PHILIPPE PROPRIÉTAIRE
APPELLATION PAUILLAC CONTROLEE
PRODUCE OF FRANCE
75 cl
TOUTE LA RÉCOLTE MISE EN BOUTEILLES AU CHATEAU

MIS EN BOUTEILLES AU CHÂTEAU

CHATEAU LAFITE - ROTHSCHILD
1955

APPELLATION PAUILLAC CONTRÔLÉE

1966

CHATEAU HAUT-BRION
PREMIER GRAND CRU CLASSÉ
APPELLATION GRAVES CONTRÔLÉE
MIS EN BOUTEILLES AU CHATEAU
DOMAINE NICHOLAS BOLÈRE S.R.A PESSAC GIRONDE

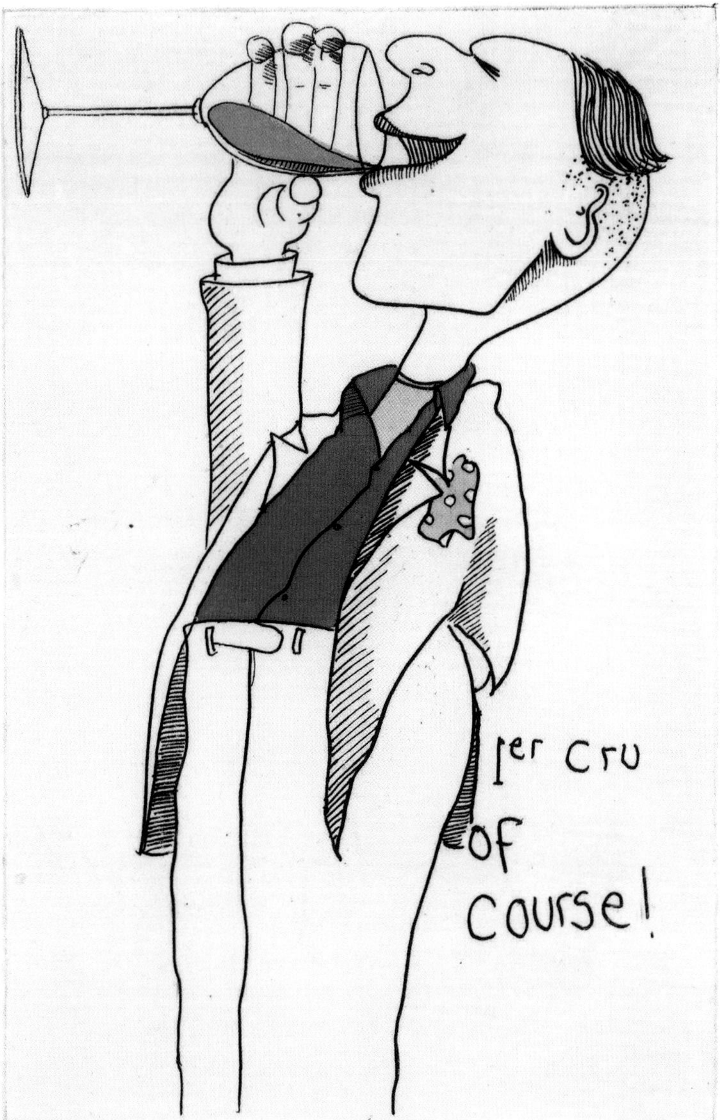
1er cru
of
course!

A.P. Life Giving Tipple! Tim

POUR IT AWAY

dear boy! You're NOT drinking A chablis with a ham sandwich!

RULE NUMBER ONE: IGNORE POMPOUS PRATS WHO LAY DOWN THE LAW ...

RULE NUMBER TWO ENJOY IT!

When I say ask an expert try your local wine merchant, they are there to help!

You don't have to dig a cellar to store your wine. Just keep away from temperature extremes (garage/shed). Under the stairs, the pantry or the mistress's knicker drawer will do!

MATURE YA LAZY BASTARDS!

Some say that excessive light + noise is bad. light perhaps but noise is questionable.

To stop corks drying + cracking up keep bottles on their sides. In aged ready to drink Port this may differ, consult an expert!

Decanting :- either stand bottle upright for two days + pour like nitro-glycerence.

or :- using a muslin to filter the dregs gently pour into a decanter. The lighted candle looks dead sexy and enables you to see inside the bottle. I've had a Latour '62 filtered through a cafetière! (bloody name dropper!)

Try not to burn your fingers!

BIFF! When opening champagne try not to go for the cheap laugh + let the cork fly into the assembled guests!

I SAY! That stung a bit!

HELP!

If you can't get invited to the right parties hide under the table and pray for spillage!

When you encounter a real stiffy (ladies! PLEASE!) Try pouring a little hot water onto the neck just to expand the glass, plunge the corkscrew clean down the middle and if necessary scream AYE KARIMBA!

NNNNG!

Beaujolais + light reds can be slightly chilled. Big Ozzie shiraz slightly warmer than a Bordeaux. Try NOT to bake them! If a little cool you can warm a recalcitrant red in the glass by hand.

ICE HOUSE   BRRRR!

We have always been told ① white, served chilled ② Red, room temperature. I wish it were as simple. Again ask an expert but basically Rieslings, Sauvignan Blancs 6-9°C, BIG Bold chardonnay 10°-12°C, cheap gear just straight from fridge!

JUST A FEW LITTLE POINTERS! (ooo...er!!)

What to serve, when to drink, what, how with which and who's whom? HELP!! Here's a little mantra I picked up :- White before red light before heavy young before old dry before sweet except when there's a vowell in the month, your girlfriend's left you and the boss has seriously pissed you off!

COLOUR

A white background is jolly helpful.

Broadly speaking lighter whites are from cooler areas + as they get older they darken. BEWARE OF A WHITE THAT'S GONE BROWN! Sweet wines are usually dark. Reds might start bright and over time lose the strength of colour. However a brown red can either be quite disgusting or totally sublime after breathing.

You've all got a cork so use it!

Use your ears mainly to sort out the bull shit!

If you smell apricots, apples, rich beautiful things like a super model's thigh then the wine should be good.

IF YOU SMELL OLD SOCK THEN POUR IT ANY WHERE BUT DOWN YOUR NECK!

Get Your Glasses Out!

Champagne flute when they say that a perfect woman's breast should fit into a champagne glass they DON'T mean this type!

Burgundy glass, very big bowl, thin, fragile but perfect for catching that big bouquet!

Perfect for Anjou wines from the Loire

Baccarat crystal. The finest glass for white or red!

long stem!

BOTTLE ANATOMY

capsule — ullage — shoulder — neck label — label — back label — strip label — punt

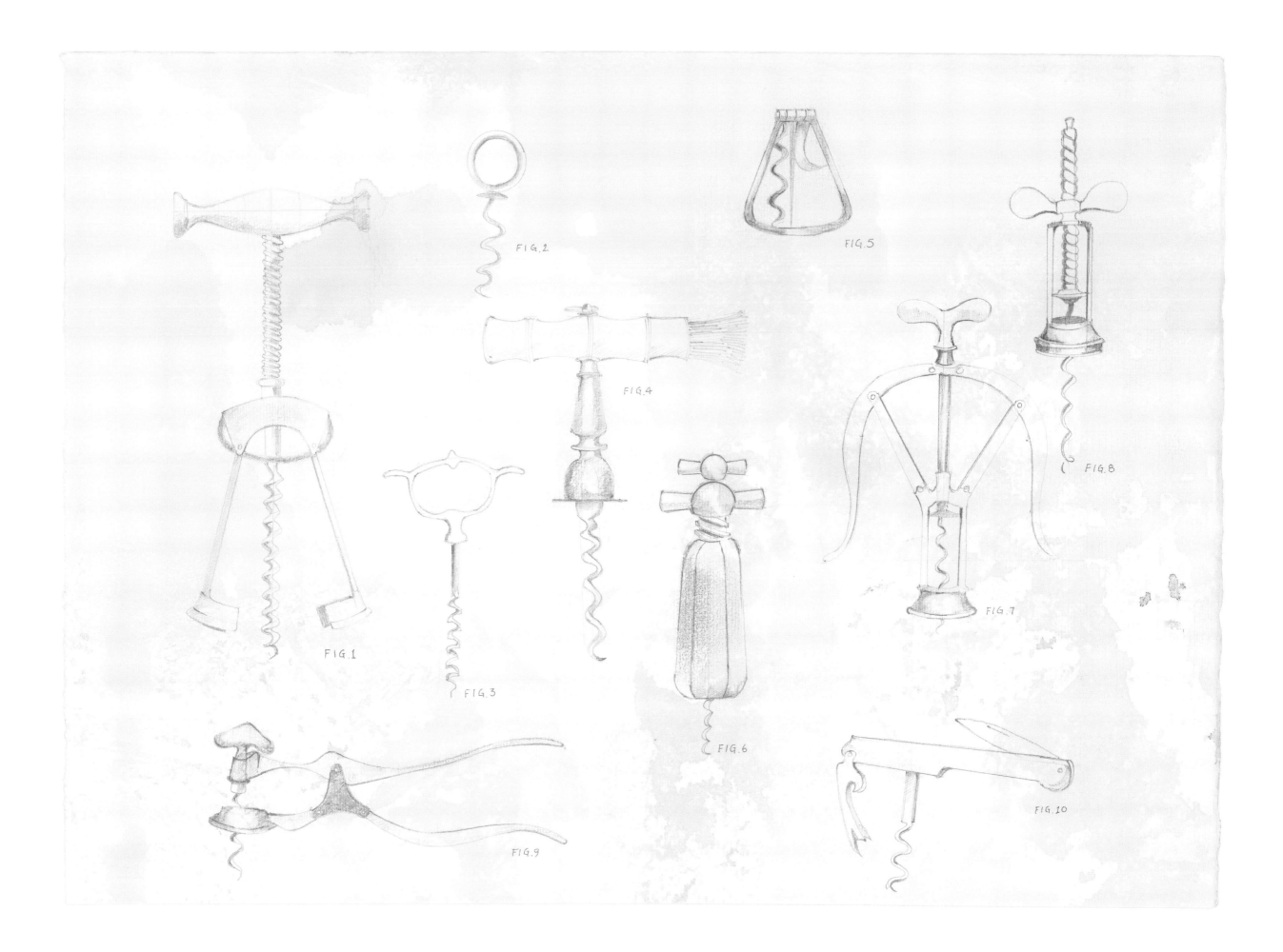

FIG.1

FIG.2

FIG.3

FIG.4

FIG.5

FIG.6

FIG.7

FIG.8

FIG.9

FIG.10

When seeking Advice WHO can You Trust?

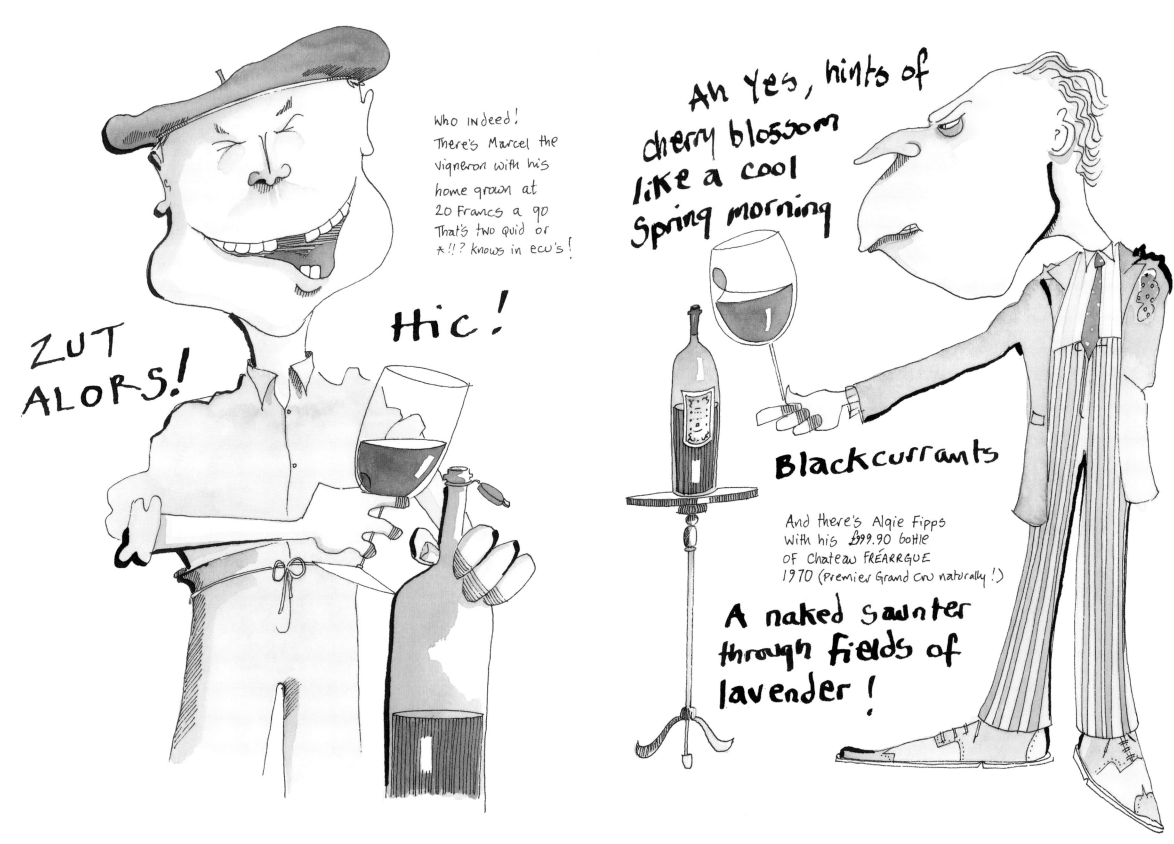

Alsace

Burgundy

Bordeaux

Clavelin

côtes de Provence

champagne

More Than
Just
Wine on
his mind!

A.P.   The old Rascal!   TiM

A.P. He came! TIM

A.P. He saw! TIM

A.P. He was conkered! TIM

A Jolly Glossary!

A.

Aerate:- To get air into the wine either by way of cleaning up an old one or softening up a naughty, brash young wine.

Grrrrr all RIGHT, all RIGHT · No need to get all aeerated!

Appellation:- literally the name. In the case of wine this informs the buyer just exactly where it hails from. A.O.C. 'Appellation d'origine contrôlée' means protected place name reserved only for the finest of french wines

er.... Je m'appelle Bert.... · phrase book

AGrafe:- The metal wire that keeps a champagne cork in place

Alcohol level:- To students and middle aged men this is the most important factor concerning wine!

The drinks are on Dad! · SOB! · BOO! HOO!

AROMA:- The gorgeous whiff of a feisty younger wine bursting to break out + bugger yer britches!

MMMMM

Astringent:- When the lining of your mouth is ripped to shreds and your tongue not only doubles in size but could easily sand down a garage door thanks to somewhat overassertive tannins + acids in a young wine.

SLOOSH!

Amplitude:- Once you've got some wine in your mouth you can then take some mental soundings. With experience you will be able to compare + describe fullness + flavour. Amplitude is a term also used in physics measuring the maximum displacement from zero or mean position of a wave or oscillation. I don't know about you but I am now totally + utterly confused!

Autolysis:- Yeast yuk which if great care is not taken will end up in the finished product. THEREFORE regular racking (changing from one vat to another) is required.

B.

Balance:- alcohol, sugar (if applicable) acid + tannin should appear in equal measure thus being well balanced.

Hi! I'm well balanced!

Barrel:- A smallish cask generally holds around sixty gallons, made of oak or chestnut. New oak barrels contain properties that flavour the wine such as vanilla but as they age they lose those properties + are sold on.

Blancs de Blancs:- champagne made solely from the white chardonnay grape.

Blanc de Noirs:- champagne made from pinot noir (red grape) without a hint of chardonnay. Quite rare!

What AM I?

Body:- As well as fullness + flavours in amplitude there is the body which signifies weight and that in turn informs the drinker as to the alcohol content.

a fuller body · MON DIEU I'AVE ZE NOBLE ROT!

Black Grape:- Red or blue grapes that are used to make red wine. Although pinot noir + pinot meunier are used to make champagne. Classic varieties include Merlot, Syrah, Cabernet Sauvignon + Grenache.

Botrytis or Noble Rot:- NO! This is not something nasty a Frenchman finds inside his undiepants. It is in fact a highly desirable mould which causes the water to evaporate + thus concentrates the sugar giving rise to the luscious sauternes dessert wines.

Beetroot nose:- purple/red mess covering the nose due to bursting capillary vessels brought on by an excess of booze and good living. See my nose in twenty years time + you'll get my drift!

BOTTOMS UP!:- A term indicating that in order to enable gravity to activate the downward forces of the wine into the mouth and down the neck one must first lift + tilt the glass in the approximate area of the mouth. This may take several years of practice so patience is required!

BOUQUET:- Ahhhhh! The smells given off by an older wine which are more subtle + complex than the aroma of a younger wine.

BRIGHT!:- A term that merely means a wine of any hue is clear of any floaty bits. However it's not all good news. Bits can be good, it's the bits that keep an old wine alive and too clean a wine could just mean that the filtration has been overdone and there ain't no goodness left in it!

Grrrrr!

BRUT:- pronounced BRUTE but NOT the same! It is a dry or dryish champagne.

BUFF!:- The best piece of advice my father in law gave me at my wedding was "ALWAYS BEWARE OF PEOPLE WHO CLAIM THEY'RE EXPERTS!" TOO BLOODY RIGHT!

C.

Case:-
a box containing twelve bottles of wine. A mixed case contains a variety and half a case contains six. A HeadCase is a Nutter who pays £10,000 for two cases of claret refuses to pay a fiver for cellarage + keeps them in his garage instead!

Château:-
literal translation means castle but in wine terms it is really only describing where the H.Q is for any particular vineyard (esp:- Bordeaux.) so it could either be some baronial pile or little more than a modest Home counties semi D'!

I SAY OLD CHAP! BANG ON!

Claret:-
The Red wines of the Bordeaux region named thus by the old English rulers in the middle ages until some clumsy sod went + lost it. Now the favored tipple of the nobs + Aristos who pronounce it thus "I say old boy, have some clear-it!"

BACK YOU GO + shoot Yourself You Imbecile!

Corked:-
It's not the wine waiter's fault! That dank, musty smell + loss of flavour is down to air finding it's way into the bottom of the cork + tainting the wine by causing mould. The cork weevil is often the guilty party. Just be polite + Alfonse will replace the bottle post-haste!

Clos:-
As in clos chaudron or clos vougeot. It means a vineyard surrounded by a wall. Enclosed. It may belong to one owner but in the case of clos vougeot up to eighty different growers own a plot + can use the name.

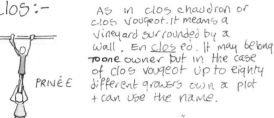

KEEP OUT   PRIVÉE

Complex:-
A wine that hits you with more questions than answers. Loads of flavours, lots of contradictions, some great things etc etc turns the noddle into scrambled egg!

CORK :-
What keeps the wine in the bottle. It is a bark that is harvested from trees mainly in Portugal + Spain. However cheaper wines are now using a plastic type cork which is perfectly adequate.

Hi! I'm yer friendly cork weevil

COARSE:-
"'ello darlin' fancy a F.. F... F... walk? Heh! Heh!" Need I say more.
A Rough, uncouth, British wine which may go down well prior to a punch up! Excellent with pasta whilst getting pissed in Pisa! I LOVE IT!!

GULP!

CRU:-
Where things start to get a bit complicated. literally means growth but then you've got premier, seconds, Troisième, Quatrièmes, Cinquièmes, Grand Cru, Cru grand bourgeois exceptionnel. It is a grading system that changes according to a wine's quality. The very finest are the Premier grand cru classés which were determined in 1855.

HOW MUCH!!

Cuvée:-
A vat or a tank. I had an uncle who drowned in a vat of Latour '61 he had to get out three times to go to the loo! BOOM! BOOM!

Girlie Mag

Cuve close or charmat Method :-
NO! NOT the chartam method (ask Spriggs mi in form III about that + it DOESN'T work!) This is the charmat method. Producing a sparkling wine by the secondary fermentation happening in the tank + not the individual bottle. It CANNOT call itself champagne.

D.

Dead:-
Frankly caput, a corpse, reddish liquid fit for nothing either too old and simply past it or maltreated as a child.

R.I.P

Let me fill you up my dear!

Decant:-
Transferring red wine into a beautiful silver topped claret jug to aerate the wine + impress the ladies or to filter off excessive sediment via a muslin. You can of course just pour very carefully from the bottle using the bit left over in the bottom for the gravy. MMM Château Palmer 1963 + giblets!

Dégorgement :-
After secondary fermentation the Lees (debris) is collected in the neck by Remuage (it's later on!) + this Yukin the neck is frozen then the bottle opened + out flies the pestilent pellet. The bottle is topped up with some wine + if required sugar, recorked + sent on its way.

 FIRE!

DOSAGE:-
I've just told you! It's when a little wine + sugar is added after the Dégorgement FAITES ATTENTION! However when it is extra brut then no sugar is added.

Depth :-
A really old, expensive, sublime, awesome Bordeaux will possess depth with an almost three dimensional flavour that pervades the soul, the spirit + the inner recesses of the mind. (Quite barking really..!!)

PUTOING!

Domaine :-
An estate which is usually referring to the Burgundy region.

Hic! Jusht another glarsh!

I said Estate NOT in a state!

D.T's:-
Delirium Tremens which is a state of shaking + trembling brought on by a life of excessive alcohol + fine living. Gout is also associated with this but you get that in your big toe.

E.

Heh! Heh!

Epinette:-
A type of scissor used for cutting grapes which can be quite lethal in the hands of an angry + embittered woman!

OW! AAARG

Etiquette:-
French word referring to the label on a bottle.
It would be fine etiquette indeed if they would only enable me to soak them off!
What do they glue them on with!

CHÂTEAU de colle
1982

F.

Hic! BURP!

ITSH REELY VERY SHIMPLE! Hic!

PROF. BOUZY

The Proshesh... Hic... Through Which ... BURP... YEAsht Reactsh ... Hic ... With Shugarsh TO FORM LUVVERLY, MARVELOUSH.... Buuuuuurp....

ALCOHOL and thush that Which turnsh.... BELCH .... GR...GR... GRAPE joosh... into ... WINE!!

FERMENTATION:-

Finesse:-

That which defines an International talent over a good county Player.

The latter has talent the former (the International that is!)

MY HERO!

has finesse which is a combination of magic, charisma + that special certain oomph! only a truly GREAT wine has finesse.

WHERE DID IT GO?

FINISH:-
The final flourish of flavour left behind after the rest of the mouthful has disappeared down the hatch. Does it linger lovingly demanding a further inspection + eventual total immersion or does it just disappear like a rude, socially inept acquaintance?

FLESHY:-

Too much fruit + not enough acidity is dull + bad news in an insubstantial wine. In a big wine however this maybe just a stage it is going through on the way to balancing out in later life.

FLYERS:-

FLYERS dear boy flyers!

IF a Wine is Bright there ain't no Flyers which are ikkle bits of stuff floatin' abaht in the bokkle!

IT'S GOT ikkle bits Floatin' Abaht!

Château de klaré

Frais:-
Cool but NOT Frozen!

I missed the world lap record by one millionth of a second? DARN it! I shouldn't have stopped half way round to comb my hair!

step any closer + I shoot!

Grand Vin:-
Bordeaux' finest. Blended from the best of the best selected cuvées only + much hand wringing, sweat + worry not to say love + tenderness goes into its creation.

G.

Grape tannin:-
every grape has its attributable features and the tannin is no exception.

oooh ah! yes I'd recognise that little monster any where!

ooooooh! cheeky!

Green:- Young + fresh like the back of a maiden's neck. Crisp, clean + pure, not unlike an old wine drinker (ahem, cough, splutter!!)

Grip:-
When the flavour clings onto the inside of the mouth. obviously if the flavour satisfies then it is most agreeable to let it hang around!

GERROFF IT'S MINE!

Grape Variety:-
Wine is made up of many types of grapes sometimes just one is used say Cabernet Sauvignan the Great Red or Chardonnay as in a thousand whites or several can be blended together such as the carignan, Grenache + Syrah grapes.

H.

ICE!

what on earth am I meant to do with a dog's hair?

Hangover:-
Drinking is fun the night before but THE FOLLOWING MORNING!! OOOF! Alcohol dehydrates the system and the brain loses the odd cell or two billion. Drink loads of orange juice and lie in a darkened room!

Harsh:-

I say! sorry old boy!

IS That What You call Wine!!

Whatever makes you blanch + wince. Can only be relieved by gripping firmly onto your host's neck!

one is full of admiration is one!

PARFAIT!

Hat:-
The skins, pips + general debris that sits on top of the juice in the vat during fermentation. It forms a layer known, funnily enough, as the Hat!

Hello Dearie fancy a little 'owsyer father!

HORS CLASSE:-
NO NOT a class whore! simply means UNCLASSIFIED As in an old harlot who's poured into her dress!

I.

Inebriated:-
A little makes you merry A lot makes you Pissed I'm crap at writing limericks but being pissed is not to be missed!

A.K.A.
Blitzed
Blootered
Buggered
Bowzered
Plastered
Pissed as a
... add chosen simile here!

J.

JUGS:-
To be admired at all times. Can also be called a Carafe and especially pleasing when filled with a well rounded local number!

K.

Kir:-
In Burgundy one can drink this sitting outside a cafe watching the world go by. It is a sweet aperitif of white wine mixed with a dash of cassis, named after Canon Kir mayor of Dijon.

Kir Royale:-
drop of cassis topped up with chilled brut champagne.

L.

Lees:-
Sediment that forms in a cask before racking (see later) or lies on the bottom side of a champagne bottle before being brought up to the neck by remuage (again see later!)

LEGS:-

Phowarrr! nice legs!

When a wine is swirled around a glass long legs or tears may appear running down the inside of the glass. This for your information is caused by ethyl alcohol + glycerine. Yeah well, You did ask!

Maceration:-

The period in which the juice of the red grapes is left to soak with skins. The longer they soak together the more colour, tannin, flavour + general scrumminess is absorbed.

NOW GET OUT before Oi Macerate Yer!

Maturation:-

This sodding Maturation process will be the death of me!

We all have to go through it I'm afraid but in wine it is somewhat more favourable. Wine matures + becomes ready for the next stage of its journey. From barrel to bottle, from bottle to merchant, from merchant to cellar, from cellar to dining room + finally ahhh! lovely!

THERE'S A MOUSSE LOOSE!

MOUSSE:-

The sparkly, frothy, fizzy bubbles in champagne + sparkling wine + how you wish to describe them. "They dance on your tongue," "struggle up the glass," "explode sending your brain into inter gallactic ecstasies!"

OLD OAK:-

After five years or so oak barrels will start to lose their oak flavours + will be sold on to be replaced by new barrels.

OAKY:-

Description of wine with woody flavour + nose. Some chardonnays for instance are over oaked. This is an indication of how important time in the barrel is. Too short is weak too long too strong.

Passerillage:-

Grapes that are left intentionally to dehydrate on the vine and will be turned into delicious sweet dessert wine. YER NOBLE ROT!

Lor! You look haggard! You want to look at yourself Darling!

Reserve:-

Riserva (It) Reserva (SP) Reserve (Bulg) Indicates a considerable time ageing before release onto the market being then supposedly of better quality (who says!) This however has no legal credibility in France.

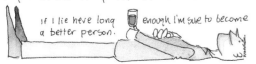

if I lie here long enough I'm sure to become a better person.

PHYLLOXERA:-

In 1863 the phylloxera vastatrix or horrible oiky little bastard aphid managed to all but destroy the entire European vine stock. It was cured by grafting the American vitis labrusca root which is immune to the pest onto the European vitis vinifera vine. GOT HIM!

Residual Sugar:-

Sugar that started its life in the grape and just won't dissolve after fermentation. Stubborn little sod!

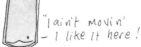

"I ain't movin' - I like it here!"

I'm SORRY to have to inform you madame that you are suffering from a very rare case of Malolactic fermentation!

Malolactic Fermentation:-

A secondary fermentation (though no more alcohol I'm afraid) in which Malic acid turns into lactic acid + carbon dioxide. In the case of champagne this is encouraged by the liquer de tirage + kept sealed in the bottle. In red wine kept loose in a barrel spillage from the bung hole is evidence of this taking place before being bunged up proper like + left to mature!

Méthode Traditionnelle:-

The champagne district very rightly defends its names + methods with hawk eyed diligence and this describes the only recognised way, same bottle secondary fermentation, in which to make proper champagne. It was known as méthode Champenoise until September 1993.

Mushroom Nose:-

Self explanatory really but an older wine may have hints of mushrooms about it especially in its bouquet. Think of a rich creamy mushroom soup and how you always take in a long, lingering whiff before enjoying the fabulous flavour!

OLD Vines:-

They don't necessarily produce a good crop + will invariably be grubbed up + replanted every 30 yrs

IF IT'S AN OLD vine it MUST be a good wine!

PUPITRE:-

Special racks, supposedly invented by Madame Clicquot with her kitchen table, which hold the bottles during Remuage in the champagne process.

Rich:-

When short of other things to say rich will cover a multitude of sins covering an abundance of flavour, tons of texture + "Hey! I'm loaded!"

Rotter:-

A barely likeable acquaintance who will worm his way into your life and before long will take up uninvited residence in your wine cellar. BE FIRM, kick him out!

Quaffable:-

Thoroughly pleasant + easy to drink.

Manzanilla La Gitana:-

NOTHING WHATEVER TO DO WITH ANYTHING IN THIS BOOK! TRY A CHILLED GLASS OF THIS GORGEOUS SHERRY ACCOMPANIED BY A LUSCIOUS YOUNG (or OLD!) PARTNER AND SOME OYSTERS. LIGHT THE BLUE TOUCH PAPER + WATCH WHAT HAPPENS!! PHOWARRR!

Mis en bouteille par:-

Carefully, lovingly + totally by hand a peasant pours your wine from the cask into the bottle aided by his doddery though nonetheless charming aged mother. There is no machinery whatsoever, RIGHT!

BOTTLING PLANT

GRAND CAMION

MUSTY:-

Doesn't have to be a bad aroma being merely slightly damp in essence BUT can resemble a smelly sock or stale cheese NOT VERY NICE!!

Oxidation:-

Effect of outside atmos' on a wine which will usually help. Sadly though a very old wine may begin to break up after a very short time.

Arggg! I'm melting... I'm melting!!

AYA SHOULD NOTTA BE INNA DIS BOOK BUT AY CUM FARROMM BARRRTH-ELL-ONA!!

Négociant:-

Whole sale merchant or trader who buys the wines in bulk + sells them on. However the Négociant Éleveur:- both makes wine + sells it. He will have his own vineyards but may buy in from elsewhere. Leading négociants in Burgundy include Louis Jadot, Bouchard et fils, Joseph Drouhin + Labouré Roi.

Roll Up! Roll Up!

PALATE:-

A.K.A MUSH, GOB, MARF, GIGGLE BOX, CHOPS

To be more precise though it applies more to the sensory side of things, the taste buds. How dull life would be without them! HEAR! HEAR!

Racking:-

Pumping the wine out from one cask into another + leaving the lees (sediment) behind.

Quaff:- Bugger the niceties get it dahn yer neck! LUVERLY!

Round:-

A young wine will have angular + irregular balance an old wine should be well rounded with all its elements in perfect harmony. (I wish!)

Ahem! While I'm still on 'R' (Just) could I mention Romanée-Conti + if you've got a bottle that you don't want just let me know. The '66 would be fine!

S.

Scented:-

subtle reminder of flowers and fruit wafting gently up the nose.
I SAID SUBTLE!

Secondary label:-
O.K so it's not as good as a first label. The grapes may not have been quite up to it but don't knock it. You can still get a well known wine but at a much more realistic price. Look out for 2000 vintage best since 1990.

LATOUR

Sediment:-
Debris + general itty bits that float about the bottle + spoil the wine if not separated out. However don't knock it thanks to those bits your 1955 Lafite still tastes BEAUTIFUL today!

I forgot to Filter!

Short:-
In an ideal world flavours would hang around a bit after swallowing but some are a little mean + illusive not wishing to stand up and be counted! They are short.

oh come on! Don't be shy!

Saucer:-
Always use a flute for champagne

O.K so the thing was apparently based on the 'Not tonight' Josephine's breast but don't serve good champagne in it. Champagne cocktail, YES! 1 cube sugar soaked in 1 drop Angostura, 2 drops cognac, slice orange 1 little red cherry then fill with champagne.

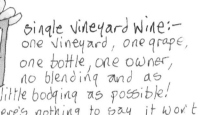
I MADE IT ALL by MYSELF. It IS VERRRRY GOOD!

Single vineyard wine:-
one vineyard, one grape, one bottle, one owner, no blending and as little bodging as possible! But there's nothing to say it won't strip the arse end off a canal barge!

oooh, lower baby lower!

SMOOTH:-
like a silken glove drawn seamlessly down a scented.... ahem... sorry...Yes where was I?...Smooth.. Well, smooth is smooth isn't it!

SNIFFTER:-
one quick drink quickly followed by another then ....another...And...!!

Sous Marque:-
Either a wine labelled under an alternative name or the lesser of the champagne houses. The labels may even appear to be totally fictitious.

PSST... Voulez vous achetez un vin sous Marque

Stems + Stalks
Stalks + Stems:-
The bit that holds the grape onto the plant and is often removed. It does however help to create tannin which is good for a longer keeping wine. It also contributes towards woody flavours. The method of stalk removal is called égrappage.

BACK IN A MINUTE GONE FOR AN ÉGRAPPAGE!

Structure:-
What constitutes the building blocks mainly in red wine.... (but sir what about white + ROSÉ... Quiet SIMPKINS!) As I was saying those basic components in a red wine are alcohol, tannin, acid + just occasionally sugar.

er..other way up chief!
RED WINE STRUCTURE PLAN!

Supérieur:-
A wine that has the added interest of a little more alcohol than is to be usually expected!

Hic!

Supple:-
To be a contortionist you have to be supple but in the case of wine supple means pleasant, accommodating, unpretentious and ultimately drinkable.
cheesie balls anybody?

Sur Lattes:-
In the champagne process the bottles end up standing upside down after Remuage 'Head in punt' prior to dégorgement.
ooof! D'you mind! can't you move across a bit!

T.

Tannin:-
better known as C76 H52 O46 but doesn't roll off the tongue quite as well! Tannic acid comes from pips, skins and stalks and gives a strong astringent bite to young wines but as I keep saying this is what will keep those rare fine wines alive for years.

SHLUUURP!

Tastevin:-
a silver tasting cup often with irregular sides and shallow to allow a clear view of the colour and the clarity. The chevaliers de Tastevins are based in Burgundy.

Terroir:-
This describes the plot and growing conditions of a vineyard or even the corner of one. Soil type, drainage, gradient, height, local geography. This is at the heart of what makes wines so different from one another.
You'll never grow vines up there!
Wanna bet on it!

Tête de Cuvée:-

The best wine produced from ANY vineyard!
FROMAGE

TEXTURE:-
How the wine feels in the mouth and whether it reminds you of a silk stocking or a sheet of sandpaper!
RASP!

Thin:-
A weak horrid all round stinker has watery insipid and general that lost any vestige of life worth living. An old wine gone well over its peak.

Tire-Bouchon:-

O.K! O.K! I know it just means bog standard corkscrew in French but this was more fun to draw
SATISFIED?!

U.

Ullage:-
The little gap of air between the bottom of the cork and the top of the wine.
Try dropping that into your next CONVERSATION!

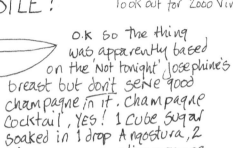

V.

Vegetal:-
Again, fairly self explanatory, a whiff that may be reminiscent of vegetation or vegetables though perhaps not a bag of spuds!

Ah yes! King Edward's three weeks old, Lincolnshire, farmer.... Fred Fullerton!

Velenché:-
A whacking great pipette that is used to transfer wine from the barrel to the glass when monitoring the maturation process.

Quick squirt anybody!

Vigneron:-
An individual who tends their own wines. Les Douze wine from Fitou is named after the 12 vignerons who contributed the grapes.

Ah! Mes filles!

Vin Clair:-
The base wine before the fizz is put into it! Not necessarily the most remarkable wine you'll ever taste on its own but after the bubbles... Oh! Bliss!

COME ON! Sparkle ya bugger!

Vin de Pays:-
A country wine, one up from vin de table, displaying the individual local characteristics free from the tight regulations required for appellation controllée.

Who pays? The Van Pays? eh?

An yes! It has a definite vinosity!

Vin de Table:-
Good honest plonk which may be at the bottom of the social wine scale but still has the required effect and no holiday would be complete without it!

Mon Dieu Vin de Table.

Ignore snotty waiters!

Vin Gris:-
A pale Rosé. (The shortest entry yet!)

YAK! YAK!

Vinification:-
The magic of turning a rather unimpressive grape juice into a glorious, wonderful, exciting not to say life enhancing substance called wine!

And I give you... WINE!

MARVO THE MAGICIAN

Vintage:-
Simply the harvest or signifies the age of when the wine was harvested. Ausone '78.

cheeky!

I SAY YOU'RE a damn fine vintage!

Vinosity:-
talk about a totally generic term that can be used without alluding to speciousness though one may be accused of a measure of blatant pedantry bordering on the merely fatuous. (Oh all right! It just means 'winey'!)

Well! stone me! waddya expect it is wine after all!

Vin Nouveau:-
A new wine as in Beaujolais Nouveau where on the 3rd Thursday in November the brand new Beaujolais is sped up to London in what was a formal race but things got a bit silly!

I'M FIRST

SMASH

CRUNCH

Vitis Vinifera:-
The most common vine on which the grapes grow. This is found throughout Europe. There are many, many more! Vitis Cinerea, Vitis Davidii, Vitis Wilsonae etc, etc, etc!!

Who on earth is he calling common?

Ignore him dear boy. The man's a peasant!

W.

Wine:-
oh come on! You can't be serious!!

Wine Bar:-
like a milk bar only you get to drink wine it it!

Wino:-
Man who is kicked out of the house but still retains his love for a fine claret.

OUT!

Could I have a glass of château Larmande old boy?

X.

'X'? An!! right! Well! Erm!... Yes here goes...
When pissed one trips over a xylophone (bloody thing!) bumps into a nasty looking xenophobe who grabs your x-rated and slams it into the Xerox (very nasty) and you are carted off in agony to the X ray dept!

Y.

Yard Arm:-
literally a bit that sticks out of a boat but the sun goes over it at six o'clock every evening whatever the season & it's time for drinkies!

Five! Four! THREE! TWO! ONE!... POP THE CHAMPERS!

YEASTS:-
teeny weeny microscopic little darlings that have a thing for sugar and they F.F... ferment together & form alcohol. What more noble thing could a micro organism do?

"Your shout!:-"
Don't take it too literally or you'll get barred! It just means that it's your turn to buy the next round!

Z.

ZINGY:-
Wines that are fresh, bright, young, attractive & vibrant.

last one in the water's a sissy!

Zonked:-
Too much of a good thing invariably ends up with.....

ZZZZZZZ

chin! chin!

Always serve chilled and upon opening
avoid aiming the bottle at innocent bystanders.
A quick shake and a careful aim should
get the creep who groped you right where it
matters!

Best served with plenty of hot water
and bath salts (and room allowing a partner of
your inclination). If you must eat something
with it then try a little caviar served on dry
toast or at most some smoked salmon.

13.5% VOL

PRODUCE OF FRANCE

Thankyou and
Goodnight!

M. Le Pee Pee

Chapter three

Passe-Temps

· · ○ ◯ ○ · ·

"Puis Je Louer du Matériel de Pêche?"

~

— That Competitive French edge ! ~

A.P.   CRUNCHED!   TiM

Chapter Four

· · · · · · · ·

La Nourriture
(Scoff!)

" J'ai pris une entrecôte, pas un tournedos! "

⸺

That other Great French Preoccupation!

Dans la cuisine !

Cassoulet

As in broth or stew the traditional French Cassoulet is as varied as you want to make it. Each cook will have their particular way of making this dish. The main ingredient which in terms of shape, size + colour is still always the bean. In Castelnaudary the Cassoulet will contain sausage and fresh salt pork; in Carcassonne a leg of mutton with a partridge when in season. The Cassoulet de Toulouse is a feast in itself containing white kidney beans, confit of goose, mutton, pork, poaching sausage, pork rind, lamb breast, goose fat, saucisses de Toulouse, garlic, tomato + breadcrumbs PHEW! I enjoyed such a dish on a baking hot day in Tuchan + was rendered helpless (or was that the bottle of wine I drank!)

Boeuf Bourguignon

Surely the best known beef dish of all time and ruined by schools + boarding houses alike. I recall it as a travesty of gristle and watery insipid gravy. The beef (Charolais say the Burgundians) should be well aged, the wine (in the Bourguignon!) should be full bodied and it should be cooked slowly until the meat is just disintegrating even further. Great Maulds

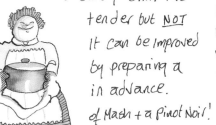

tender but NOT it can be improved by preparing a day or more in advance. of mash + a Pinot Noir!

Andouillettes

I have enjoyed Andouillettes in Troyes where they produce the finest. As delicious as they are the ingredients don't make for the prettiest of reading! First find the small intestine of a pig, mix it with parts of the stomach of a calf or anything else for that matter and stuff it! serve with frites.

Edible Fungi

Fabulous in OMELETTE

grisette

cep

Always advisable to consult an expert before eating weird fungi!

Fairy Ring champignon

Field mushroom

Parasol

A Few MAJOR Dishes

a pig, a that

Not that sort of dish you fool!

WHITING

A MODEST LITTLE BANQUET

Elizabeth David (Bow, scrape, grovel) describes how in 1949 while struggling with rationing the Big cheeses of the Burgundy Wine Federation sat down to a banquet of Boudin + Andouillettes with Dijon Mustard, sucking pig in jelly flavoured with Mersault, Pouchouse (fish) in a sauce of pounded garlic, a haunch of wild boar with a rich grand veneur sauce and potato croquettes and just to fill up a little more space roast chicken + a wide variety of cheeses. The pudding was Biscuit Argentin (The Argentine Ambassador was there!) WINES!! Aligoté from Mersault, Beaujolais '48, two more from Côte de Beaune, three classics from Nuits Saint Georges (Vougeot + Musigny) + a sparkling Burgundy from the Côte de Nuits. The liquers were Marc + Prunelle (if that's anything to do with Prunes I bet they needed it!!)

Salade Niçoise

A classic French salad with all my favourite ingredients.
FOR FOUR TAKE:-
6 tomatoes, 6 eggs, 8 anchovy fillets, 2 sweet peppers, 2 slices ham, 3½ oz olives, salt, pepper, 3 table spoons oil to 1 of vinegar. Hard boil eggs, let cool, peel, cut into quarters. In dish arrange quarters of egg and tomato, chopped peppers, pieces of diced ham + olives. Prepare well seasoned vinaigrette. SERVE!

Bouillabaisse Marseillaise

Pronounced BWEE a base Marce ay aze. The classic Mediterranean staple which horny handed men of the sea eat because there's sod all else and rich tourists hunt out exhaustively in an effort to find that one true authentic flavour of the sea. No doubt the latter pay a fortune and the former think them stupid but will take them out on their boats for 2000ff and sell them their Grandmothers' recipe for a further 500ff! Basically the greater the variety of fish used the better just as long as they swim in the Med. White fish might include bass, red mullet, John Dory, whiting, monkfish, scorpion fish, perch and haddock while the rest may feature eels both Conger + Moray, mackerel and striped bass. Shell fish such as lobster might impress the tourists but the fisher folk would only take a break in an almighty punch up to fillet the chef responsible!!

OMELETTE

Soldat ou marmite

I believe in all modesty that I make the finest scrambled egg in the Northern hemisphere. However I keep meeting people who harbour the same conviction of their superiority in the scrambled egg stakes. Omelette produces the same reaction, although in my house Sarah does the omelette! Here are a few pointers:-
① don't beat eggs to death, stir gently with a fork.
② don't over do the filling, the egg is king.
③ use a decent pan.
④ season with a little salt + pepper.
⑤ don't go mad with the heat.
⑥ GO BABY GO!

COQ AU VIN

The perfect end for an old bird who's way beyond laying. A tough sinewy old cock or hen needs a good marinade to tender up + reinvigorate the old meat. In this instance the bird needs jointing into more manageable pieces before complete immersion in the marinade. To prepare the marinade mix red wine, onion, carrot, celery, bouquet garni, garlic, peppercorns + olive oil. Boil up the mixture, simmer for five minutes and leave to cool. The meat should be left in the marinade for a good six hours before taking out and patting dry on some paper towel. Now the REAL work begins. Heat up some oil + butter in a pan and brown 1/4 lb of bacon, take out and whack in chicken skin side down, brown, turn over + remove. Chuck in 15 baby onions (x. cruel!) and slightly brown, take THOSE out and add 1/2 lb quartered mushrooms + again sauté + remove. O.K SO FAR? Now, keep back just two table spoons of the fat and add the onion, carrot + celery (1 of each by the way!) from the marinade + cook gently until soft but NOT brown. Sprinkle 2/3 oz flour + cook until bubbly + foamy. Stir in the rest of the marinade + 3/4 pint of broth and add the chicken along + 1 clove crushed garlic, 2 chopped shallots, bouquet garni + salt + pepper. Simmer for up to 1 hour until the bird is tender. Put the baby onions into a casserole dish and strain sauce over them + simmer for ten minutes. Add mushrooms and simmer for a couple of minutes. Return chicken and bacon to the sauce. Serve from the casserole dish. Straight forward? well-ish!!

Just who do you think you are calling an old cock!

oo in'e LUVLY!

Longe d'Agneau aux herbes

Tomates farcies aux Champignons

Potée Auvergnate

Gâteau aux pêches et aux framboises

Gâteau au Pample Mousse

Calf's Head Vinaigrette

Now here's one to serve up for the mother in law! I have no intention of ever tackling this but I just love the recipe. first of all go to your butcher and ask for one Calf's head (I don't think you'll find one lying around!) Ask him to bone it and tie it (he's sure to thank you!) Once you've got the thing home scoop the brains out and soak before

GULP!

soaking the head itself overnight change water the next day + bring to the boil wiping off any scum + scraping

away any unsightly hairs from the snout. Oi SLAP HER! THE LADY IN THE FIFTH ROW'S JUST FAINTED! Bring a fresh sauce pan of water to the boil with a couple of carrots + onions. Place the head in this and simmer for 10-15 minutes. It MUST be totally submerged, stay on scum watch. Add salt, wine vinegar, parsley, celery and olive oil. Cover + simmer for 90 minutes. Back to the brains. SHE'S GONE AGAIN! Free brains of skint blood (lots of soaking + changing of water!) prepare a court-bouillon of 1 3/4 pints water, tablespoon salt, 1 onion, 2 tablespoons white wine vinegar + bouquet Garni. Simmer this for 1/2 hour. Cool it + strain. Poach brains in this gently for 15 mins. Take out the head and serve on a very hot dish. I for one have a sudden craving for chicken nuggets + chips. But Hey! Each to his own! IS THE LADY ALRIGHT NOW? oh good!

CRÊPES DENTELLES

WE WONT TO KOOK!

You could do this fun little recipe with the little darlings on a rainy afternoon when the F.A.Cup semi final is on telly, your wife has just found a strange pair of knickers in your brief case and you still have the remnants of a foul hangover from the previous week end.

Ingredients. 2 large Eggs, 4 oz butter, 4 oz Flour, 4 oz sugar, 1/4 pint milk, table spoon of rum (Dad to finish off bottle) + salt.

Stir eggs, flour, sugar, pinch of salt, rum + some just melted butter until quite smooth, slowly stir in the milk until creamy. Grease a heavy iron pan very lightly with butter. Put it over heat and add the mixture one table spoonful at a time. Turn over, take out and serve with melted butter + sugar. Kids make a filthy mess, Dad rants + raves, Mum hugely amused offers to tidy up and cook Calf's head Vinaigrette as a special treat!

COGNAC, ARMAGNAC, MARC AND CALVADOS

Cognac started out as crap wine which was boiled up out of desperation and Wow! became Magic spirit! Armagnac is similar, from Bordeaux + distilled just the once. Marc is not made from grapes but from the Burgundian wine pulp. Calvados is made from Normandy Apples. All of these can be sublime or strong enough to decoke an old boiler!

ESCARGOTS

Head of the Escape Committee!

In a nutshell they're easy to catch but a bugger to clean. Their getaway technique still needs a little work!

In order to render them palatable just follow these straightforward directions.

① Starve the poor mites for five days
② On sixth day give them a little flour
③ On seventh day soak them in water for ten minutes
④ If they don't pop out to thank you for the diet then discard the ungrateful little brutes (they're dead I'm afraid)
⑤ Pop the live ones into a container and mix in a little coarse salt which will bring out the yucky goo!
⑥ Rinse thoroughly
⑦ Simmer for two hours in a pot of water flavoured with white wine, thyme, bay leaf, salt and peppercorns.
⑧ Whip 'em out of their shells, extricate their bellies and the tough end bit.
⑨ Promise yourself that next time you'll buy them pre prepared from the supermarket.

The best snails will be found in any vineyard especially in Burgundy. 'Escargots de Bourgogne' cooked in garlic flavoured batter + fried in oil YUMMY!

Tweety Birds

We English tend to be somewhat squeamish as regards the mass destruction of small birds for the table. Some are disguised in pâté like the larks of Pithiviers or served for all to see on a croûte of bread.

BLAM!

They are generally seared with innards intact + eaten whole. Sparrows, thrushes and blackbirds can also find themselves on a French country dinner table. An acquired taste I'm sure.

A Little HARD —

GULP!

MENU Le RESTAURANT DE LA RÉPUBLIQUE

CORE GASTRONOMY

Hang on don't rush!

May I take ze Liberté of rrrecommending ze Frogs legs followed by ze leetle bird on ze toast cooked in ze innards wizze 'ead still attached and to follow 'ow about a lovely beeg Horsey steak cooked verry rare wiz ze joooses mixing with shallots and aubergines, garlic + onion. To finish perhaps our spécialité Gateau du chocolat and double cream!

FROGS

We have always been told that frogs legs taste like chicken. Doesn't everything according to Mothers, Matrons and Maiden Aunts! However, covered in white wine, garlic and herbs they are, apparently, delicious. In the Massif Central region they are deep fried. Frog is rarely seen on a menu these days and the job of frog catcher is currently vacant. They call us 'Roz Beefs' we call 'em f..f..f..fine Gentlemen!

Heh! Heh! Sucker!

PUTOING!

HORSE of COURSE!

THIS WAY!

The English have always considered the eating of horse flesh as being totally barbaric + inhumane but then again the French don't pack their children off to boarding school at eight! The Anglo Saxons used to sacrifice horses and weren't averse to eating them. Once Christianity began to be imposed on the tribes it was deemed prudent to ban entirely the eating of horseflesh so as to deter any further sacrifice to Woden. The French have always considered horse as a good substitute for beef and there was a time when it was considerably cheaper as old farm horses would end up in the pot. An old nag will still produce good meat unlike an old cow. Ordinary butchers used to close on a Monday but the horse butcher stayed open thus Monday was horse meat day. Old habits die hard. Most horse meat is now imported.

You don't need any help from me to look stupid!

Make me look stupid again + it's the burger van for you old boy!

FOIE GRAS

Geese are force fed grain thus artificially and unnaturally enlarging their livers. The Romans did it with figs (I don't know what they did with the geese though!) Foie Gras like Truffles is seen as a rich man's treat. A whole pâté can be baked in brioche or quickly flipped in sizzling butter and served with noodles. It can be bought in cans but to serve this to the connoisseur would produce howls of protest. I'm not sure how the poor goose feels about this!

OYSTERS

← ramekin

There are two main types of oyster, flat & hollow which if kept in close proximity will cause a dreadful scene and protest in the strongest terms! The oyster aficianado much prefers the flat variety. This includes the famous Belon from Rieuc-sur-Belon in southern Brittany. They can be absolute buggers to open so creep up on them double quick before they notice and tackle 'em hinge end first with the appropriate knife. A platter of mixed oysters with a chilled dry white wine is simply SUPERBE ET FORMIDABLE! Mind you ladies beware brylcremed cads bearing oysters and champagne!

Ow about a leetle snack my dear!!

Heh! Heh!

GARLIC

lovely with lamb dishes, fish, beef oh ANYTHING!

Researchers have just discovered what the french have known for centuries that garlic is actually good for you. Every meat & two veg Brit thinks that every Frenchman reeks of garlic. This may be true but then if we had more garlic we'd not only be healthier but then nobody would notice the smell either! In order of strength the weakest is white followed by violet & red'll knock your block off! If a clove is firm & plump then it is young & fresh!

PHOOO-ORE!

GARLIC is wonderful & should be used with extravagant abandon but can be a deterrant when trying to attract the opposite sex!

TRUFFLES

Legend surrounds this mysterious underground fungus that can only be sniffed out by trained porkers. It is priced way beyond the reach of us ordinary mortals! A whiff of truffle is sublime but stick your nose into a paper bag full of truffles and you may assume to have stuck your nose into the armpit of a large, fat, hairy, sweaty man who is currently collecting towels in a Turkish Bath. They tend to lose their flavour after a week so if not eaten straight away they can be brushed clean & preserved in cognac or Madeira. The finest French truffles are to be found in Périgord & Quercy. Truffles like oysters are said to be aphrodisiacs but then I can't afford either to find out!

SOME FINE FRENCH SCOFF

a Hachoir

a sauteuse

Exhibit 'A'

poëlon

YUM! YUM!

How to avoid streaming eyes when preparing onions!

DU PAIN

← chinois

The average British household considered bread either fit only for toasting or left to go stale only to end up on the bird table. fortunately the notorious white sliced mass produced pulp is being put under pressure by far more tasty, unusual and healthy options many of which have come from Europe. In France the first job of the day may be to call in at the boulangerie to collect the family baguette. This will be caked in delicious jam to accompany the first coffee of the day or will wipe the platter clean after a cassoulet. It will be eaten with pâté, or served floating on soup. It is truly ubiquitous!

The Baguette is a bothersome bugger to bake!

French breads include
pain de campagne
pain complet
pain de seigle (rye)
Pain Flomande
Gâche
Faluche, etc. etc!!

Shallots & ONIONS

These vegetables are actually related to the lily family (as are leeks, garlic & chives.) The old name for the shallot was onion of Ascalon. Purple shallots are considered the finest. onions are generally stronger in flavour and are beautiful sautéed gently in butter. A good shallot recipe is La Daube Santongeaise (beef stew with carrots!) As you know if in doubt whack an onion in! Thick onion soup is sublime!

Mustard

Mustard comes from Dijon and in 1382 the Duke of Burgundy granted a coat of arms with the motto 'Moult Me Tarde' which means 'Much Awaits Me!' thus MOUTARDE geddit! Any dish which has 'à la Dijonaise' in the title contains guess what!! Mustard grains are ground into the juice of sour grapes (verjus) into which are added herbs & spices etc. It is also considered a remedy for any amount of ailments from asthma to the runs!

Dijon Moutarde

A.P.   Escargots   Jim

A.P   Bon Appetit!   Tim

A Potted History

We all have our favourite cheese though strangely for some reason we recoil on seeing a little bit of mould on a crust or whiffing a cheesy sock but will readily lunge at a reeking Roquefort which is in essence a glorious lump of mould and smell. Cheese comes in every shape, size, texture and flavour and it is made from the milk of cows, goats, sheep, mares, well any mammal that lactates should be able to produce cheese but I think we'll leave that one there! Cheese can be hard, soft, blue, crumbly and as runny as a toddler's nose. It requires just one major ingredient GOOD MILK from cows (etc!) fed not on processed feed but good, lush pasture. An Alpine Meadow may not produce much milk but the FLAVOUR! The French produce about 800 different cheeses and it all started with Roquefort over 2,000 years ago. It's production, as with wine & spirits, was down to the monasteries who passed on their knowledge to local farmers. Every region now has its own particular cheese determined by the lay of the land and the climate, as with wine it is sensitive to its own terroir (type of soil, drainage, shade, climate etc!)

every chef loves his cheese!!

Boursin

Wrinkly Wrapper!

Just to start the ball rolling this first cheese is probably appearing on a dinner table near you tonight but it wasn't in fact created until 1957. It is a creamy cow's milk cheese that is mixed with herbs and comes in an attractive crinkly wrapper. It was devised by (surprisingly enough!) M. Boursin.

DU VIN DU PAIN ET DU BOURSIN

Remember the advert!

"CHEESE!"

Souffle Risen! Souffle Sunk!

PHUT!

chabichou is not generally worn as a hat!

Camembert de Normandie

O.K so I'm hardly pushing the boat out in terms of being adventurous but these cheeses to use the modern vernacular deserve to be 'BIGGED UP' (ghastly expression!). During the French Revolution Mme Harel took in a priest and he had worked with farmers in the Brie area. This is the Harel's interpretation of it. It is delicious served naked on a dry water biscuit accompanied by a good Beaujolais.

BY serving naked I mean without butter but hey! Each to his own!

Chabichou Du Poitou

Is that eclectic enough for you? It is a goat's milk cheese that comes from Poitou a marshy region near La Rochelle just north of Bordeaux. It is a cylindrical cheese that has a bluish grey mould over and above the first layer of thin white mould. A firm creamy texture that grills beautifully

Laruns

From the Pyrénées

Now we get amongst the hard stuff! This is a hard unpasteurised sheep's milk cheese. A flat wheel in its uncut state with a yellowish natural rind best eaten when young. Like all things young it is pliant (ooh er Missus!) However after six months it becomes craggy like the cantankerous old shepherd's who make it!

Brie de Meaux

This is surely the most famous of the classic soft white cow's milk cheeses in France. It has a white, yellow rind that bears the marks of the straw matting on which it is matured. The cheese itself is smooth with an irresistible hint of mushrooms. When made from the indigenous cow's milk then it is supreme but all too often it borders on the bland when made from the milk of the all too common Friesian.

oi! Who are you calling common. Just plain popular that's all!

P.S. It's from the Ile de France

Mimolette Française

The real cheese nut may be aware that this cheese originated in the Netherlands but that was probably when Flanders was part of Holland. Anyway it's French now o.k! It is a hard cow's milk cheese with a rind ranging in colour from a yellowy orange to light brown. It is shaped like a ball and as tough as old boots. When I last had some I hovered between a jack hammer and ½ lb of semtex by way of chipping a bit off. It has a very strong lip numbing flavour. Best served with light French Ale, LOTS OF IT!

caprice des dieux

rollot

pavé d'Affinois

neufchâtel

Le Brin

Le Roulet

Pélardon

Please ignore that chap trying to chip away at his Mimolette. This cheese is a totally different prospect altogether. Pélardon comes from Languedoc-Roussillon and is a traditional, unpasteurised farmhouse Goat's milk cheese.

It is softer than most in the Goat collection with a creamy consistency and a salty after taste. It hardens with age but still retains a creaminess in the mouth.

It's thin + wrinkled with a white + blue mould!

Raclette

shit! We've escaped onto the wrong page

keep going no one's noticed!

Great Après Ski TREAT!

From the Mountains of Savoie a great wheel of semi soft cow's milk cheese with a pink natural rind. It is usually cut in half placed on a special stand + stood near a flame. As the cheese begins to melt it can be dripped onto anything you fancy but steaming spuds are very nice smothered in a glorious layer of nutty, fruity melted mountain cheese.

Cold Meat →

Selles-sur-cher

A classic Goat's milk cheese from the Loire. Small rounds of perfect chèvre (Goat's milk cheese) with ash covered rind and in slightly older cheeses a bluey grey mould. The Loire is the French centre for Goat's milk cheese so get out there! They come in every shape known to man + will melt the hardest heart. It is also glorious when melted onto salad.

MY little PRoblem with GoAT's Cheese!

I've always had such a lovely time with Goat's cheese until recently when I've had one or two with that horrid sort of soggy goat's arse and wet dog flavour. In my researches (cheese for twits 1953) I have discovered why this is. Goats' milk is very sensitive and if not treated with all due care tiny fat globules burst and release that horrid flavour into the cheese. They should be allowed to break down gradually + enhance the flavour not ruin it. HANDLE YOUR NANNY WITH CARE!!

TOO MUCH cheese can cause WEIRD DREAMS!

Vignotte

Now this, I have to confess, is one of my favourites. Like Brie, Boursin + camembert it can be found on most Deli counters in the land. This is a soft white traditional cow's milk cheese from Champagne + Lorraine. It has a smooth rind and a succulent flavour with hints of lemon + salt. It is VERY moreish and once started it won't let go!

I LOVE CHEESE ME!

The old Cheese PRESS! CREAK GROAN

CURDS AND WHEY HAY HAY!

I am flirting with danger and grave uncertainty on this one. Cheese making is as complex or as simple as any one producer wishes to make it. Some are created as if by sleight of hand from the Heavens and others through years of careful, analytical and methodical research. If you visit a cheesemaker he'll or of course she'll maybe even they'll show you what he, she or they want you to see but like as not there'll be a vital part of the operation that is a jealously guarded secret. I shall attempt all too inadequately I'm afraid to describe a little bit of the procedure. For soft cheeses unpasteurised milk is allowed to go off + in order to speed up the process + avoid bitterness a portion of the previous day's milk is added (the starter) to speed up the coagulation. Enzymes react with fats and proteins then after much stirring, draining, adding of this + removing of that Hey Presto a soft white cheese. (told you it was rubbish!) As for hard cheese a rennet must be added which is a natural enzyme from all milk fed babies that divides the milk into whey or liquid that is drawn off and curds that contain the fats + proteins or solids which form the basis for a hard cheese that will withstand time and mature thus enabling the stranded shepherd to survive the long cold winter in his mountain refuge with his internet + cellphone!

La classe ouvrière   The Relais Routier ~ Wholesome fare!

Chapter Five

· · ○ ○ ◉ ○ ○ · ·

La Bataille des Sexes!

"Avez-vous mal là?" — "Oui c'est Mon Mari!"

~ a little Well natured skirmish of the sexes! ~

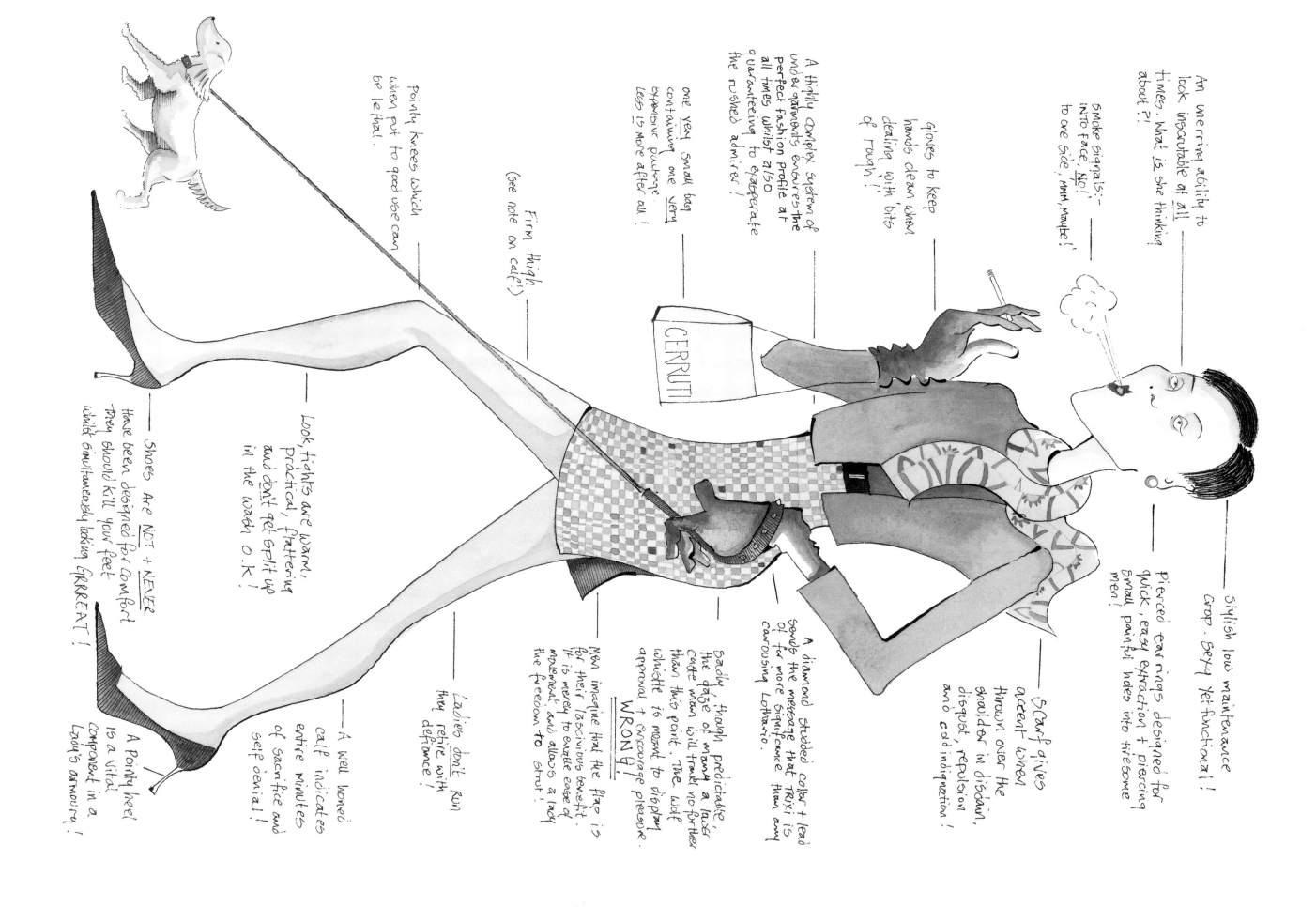

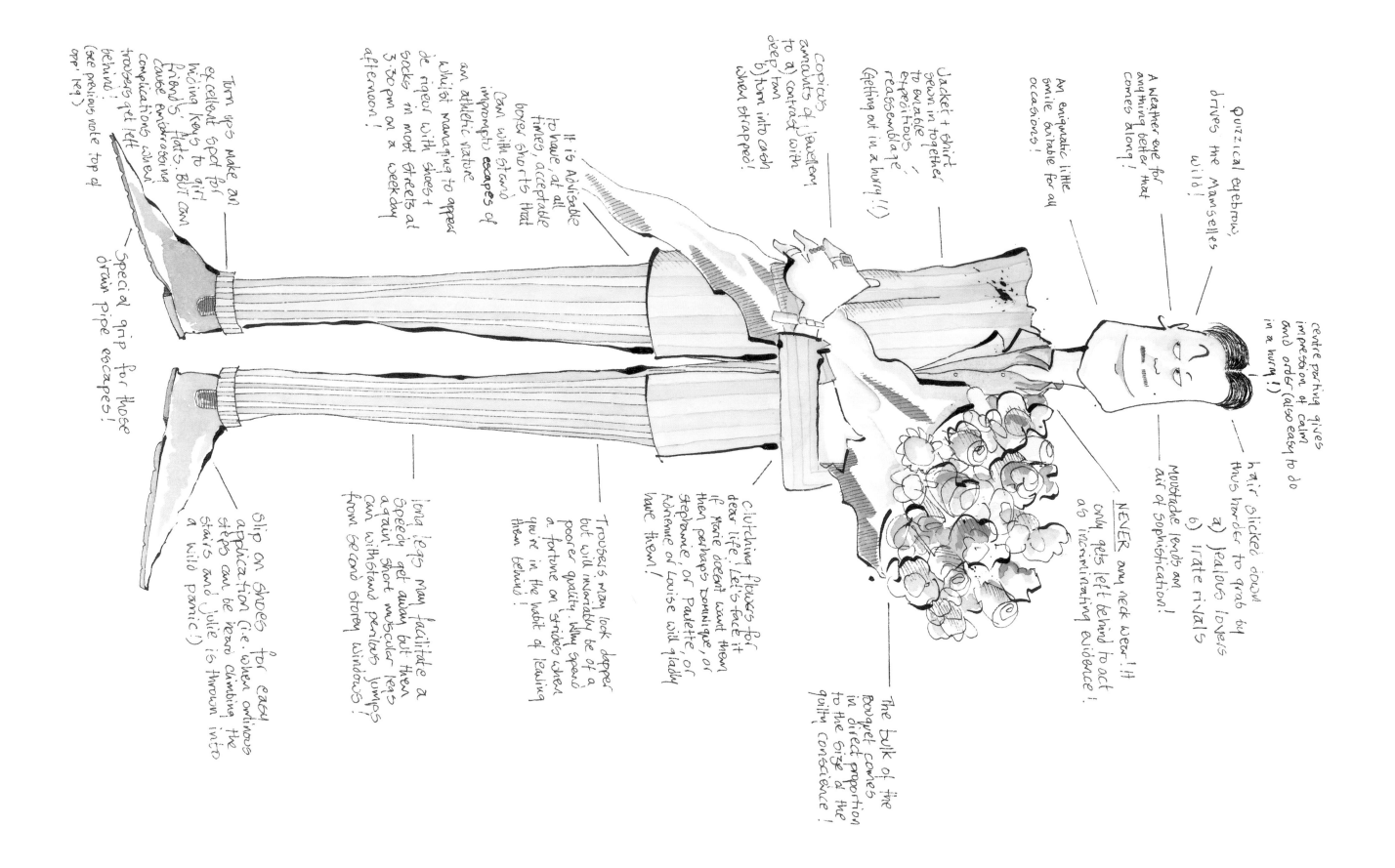

That old chestnut!

Fait Accompli!

SORTING OUT
The Wheat from
the chaff!

Well, let's face it, he gets to enjoy seeing
you in all the stuff!

Chapter Six

· · · · ○ · · · ·

· Les Autos ·

"Pouvez-vous nettoyer le Parebrise, s'il vous plaît?"

A Celebration of Some Great French Marques

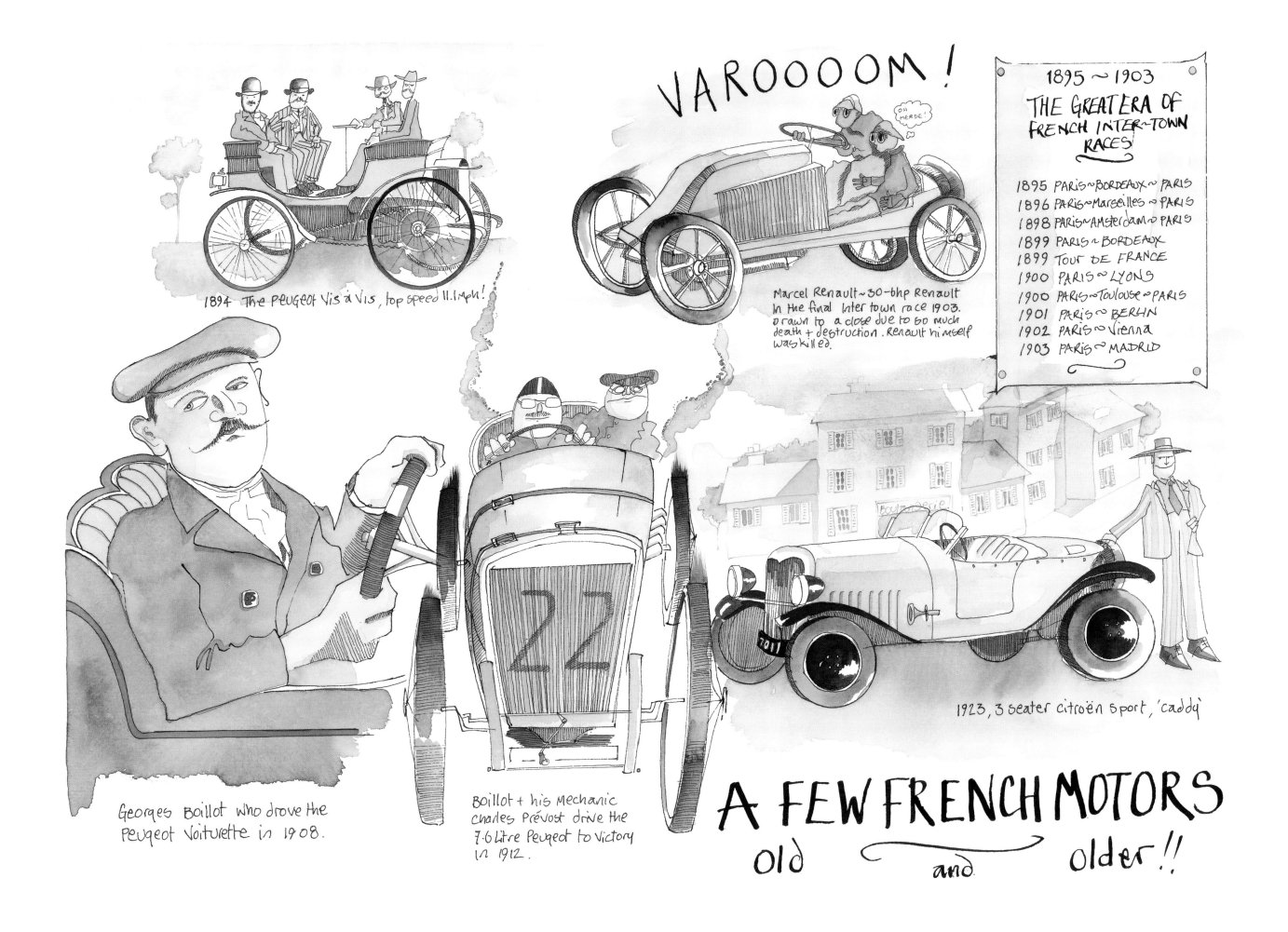

VAROOOOM!

OH MERDE!

1895 ~ 1903
THE GREAT ERA OF
FRENCH INTER~TOWN
RACES

1895 PARIS ~ BORDEAUX ~ PARIS
1896 PARIS ~ Marseilles ~ PARIS
1898 PARIS ~ Amsterdam ~ PARIS
1899 PARIS ~ BORDEAUX
1899 TOUR DE FRANCE
1900 PARIS ~ LYONS
1900 PARIS ~ TOULOUSE ~ PARIS
1901 PARIS ~ BERLIN
1902 PARIS ~ Vienna
1903 PARIS ~ MADRID

1894 The Peugeot Vis à Vis, top speed 11.1mph!

Marcel Renault ~ 30-bhp Renault in the final Inter town race 1903. Drawn to a close due to so much death + destruction. Renault himself was killed.

Georges Boillot who drove the Peugeot Voiturette in 1908.

Boillot + his Mechanic Charles Prévost drive the 7.6 Litre Peugeot to victory in 1912.

1923, 3 seater citroën sport, 'caddy'

A FEW FRENCH MOTORS
old — and — older!!

The 1937 Légère Citroën. The lack of a roof caused structural weakness + it was honourably discharged in 1939.

1920's, the Citroën 5CV

SACRE BLEU! MON DIEU! C'est impossible!

1948 the first appearance of the legendary Citroën 2CV.

People may deride it but how many cars are still driven today that are basically unchanged over 50 yrs?

The sleek, stylish and sexy Citroën DS 23 Pallas, 1973.

André Citroën 1878-1935

RENAULT 4 : A classic

1979 Jean Pierre Jabouille wins the French Grand Prix at Dijon in a Renault. René Arnoux was third

D.S 23

A.P   The Tin Snail   Tim

2 CV !
à la plage !

A.P.   Light Fantastic   JM

La traction Avant

Chapter Seven

· · · · · · · ·

· Un Peu d'Histoire! ·

"Après Moi le deluge!" - "Qu'ils Mangent de la Brioche!"
"Liberté, Egalité, Fraternité!" - "Oh, Josephine, Je suis fatigué!"

∞

A bolt through five thousand Years of French History and a few famous French faces!

· · · · · O · · · ·

A History of France: Part one!

4760 B.C. Megalithic culture in Brittany

Birth of the Art critic!

"It has a certain raw energy, an overbearing honesty, that I find irresistable!"

DAD! Why's she talking total Bollocks?

911

1066

451 A.D THE MEROVINGIANS

476

oi Atilla! look up THERE mate.

WHA—!!

URGH!

SQUELCH

I'm off then... er... Well.. bye... O.K. be seeing you.... cheerio.. PIP-PIP... Must dash er... Bye... Hello?... I'm off Home to Rome sod you then!

ROME

The fall OF THE ROMAN EMPIRE

YER! SOD OFF! What did you lot ever do for us!!

58-52 BC Helmets, swords + shields

THE START OF THE ARMS RACE!

Julius caesar's Gallic Wars

You've let me down you scumbag!

You're strangling me!!

He was tall, stocky, very strong + charismatic He went from Duke to become King OF ENGLAND.

William Duke OF NORMANDY

TREATY OF St-clair-sur-epte. Charles The Simple + The Viking chief Rollo CREATE THE DUCHY OF NORMANDY

1194 to 1260 Chartres Cathedral Built

MEROVIUS KING OF THE SALIAN FRANKS DEFEATS ATILLA THE HUN

AY KEN not see a darn SING AARG!

TAKE THAT, MUSH. Oi! URGG!

1337-1453 The 100 Years War. ENGLISH Plantagenets ·V· French Capetians. ALL to do With DISAGREEMENTS OVER ACCESSION of French Throne

Now You've got The thing finished could you PLEASE get on With Tiling my bathroom!

(Sharp intake of breath) it'll have to be Tuesday week I'm afraid!

OH GOD OF BATTLES! Steel My soldiers' hearts..... I say dear boys keep it down I've got to go through My lines You know!

Henry V

Come + Fight You cowards!

Run for it The french Bird's Barmy!

Joan D'Arc Recaptures Orleans ~ 1429

Henry VIII OF ENGLAND

Francis I OF FRANCE

I think you'll find I'm considerably richer than you!

AYE SINK NOT!

1520 A little bit of ostentatious POSTURING AT The Field of The cloth of Gold at Guines (NOT FAR from the channel Tunnel!)

ZZZZZ

1541 Calvin Publishes his 'Institutes of The Christian Religion' first Great classic of French literature. YET TO BE TURNED INTO A MUSICAL!

"A DARN GOOD READ!" The Daily Zealot

THEY'RE AT IT AGAIN!!

CLAAK! BIFF! AAAARGH! THUD!! OOOF! CRASH! BOFF! THOK NYUK YIKES! AIEEEE!

'Catholics to the left, Protestants to the right, France in the middle. Nobility upset the applecart. Blood, confusion, Massacre, assassination, persecution, corruption.....

MAY YOUR GOD GO WITH YOU!

1562-1598 The Wars of Religion (Religion, I ask you!!)

The Bourbons (NO! NOT The Biscuits!)

LOUIS XIII 1610-1643

Henry IV **1589-1610** took throne as a Protestant but in order to bring about Peace became a Catholic. (It sometimes pays to be a little expedient!)

1610

ASSASSINATED BY A RELIGIOUS FANATIC "TWAS EVER THUS!"

1637 Descartes Publishes his "DISCOURSE ON METHOD" "COGITO, ERGO SUM" I Think Therefore I am

"WOOF! It blew My Mind!!" philosophy TODAY

LOUIS XIV 1643-1715 "The Sun King" Built Versailles DEFEATED SPAIN

MONARCHY GOES A BIT OFF AND THE PEASANTS GET QUITE REVOLTING!

I think we'll have a canal....erm.... THERE!

PANT, GASP! AND THEY'LL ALL SAY HE built this sodding canal!!

R.. R..!

DID You Know That Henry IV built this bridge? WHAT... on his own!

Henry was a Great Builder + made Huge IMPROVEMENTS TO THE NATIONAL INFRASTRUCTURE

Cardinal Richelieu **1585-1642** Power broker, schemer, underpinned the throne built the navy, encouraged overseas expansion

1635 Founds Académie Francaise which now forbids words such as Le weekend + L'Hovercraft!

1782 THE MONTGOLFIER BROTHERS In first HOT AIR BALLOON flight

VIVE LA REVOLUTION!

Louis XV followed by Louis XVI Then Aaaaaaargh!

Joan of Arc

RUN AWAY!

She inspired the French with her religious zeal during the 100 years War against England. In 1431 she was captured by the English + burned at the stake.

Coco Chanel

She liberated French women in the 1920's by creating clothes with 'chic'. Like Joan she is a true French heroine.

SPLAT!

Toulouse Lautrec 'Ringside'!

Rodin Makes necessary Adjustments!

Louis Pasteur discovers the rabies virus in 1881 and by 1885 has introduced inoculation

1903 Marie + Pierre Curie win the Nobel Prize for their research into Radioactivity

Jacques Tati

Gentle Genius

Jour de Fête
Les Vacances de M. Hulot
Mon oncle
Playtime
Traffic

The Modern
world disconcerted
him so he
'sent it up'
showing us all
what a vacuous
set up Modernity
can be!

!

From an era when Rugby players
drank, smoked,
stayed up all night
Carousing then
thrashed the opposition
the following afternoon!

Jean-Pierre Rives

A favourite among a
feast of phenomenal French
Flankers!

Alain Prost

Known as
'The Professor'
he had one
of the finest
brains on the
Formula one
circuit.

VAROOOOM

Victory at Spa Francorchamps
in 1983 in the Renault RE40.
The Rest of the field are nowhere
to be seen!

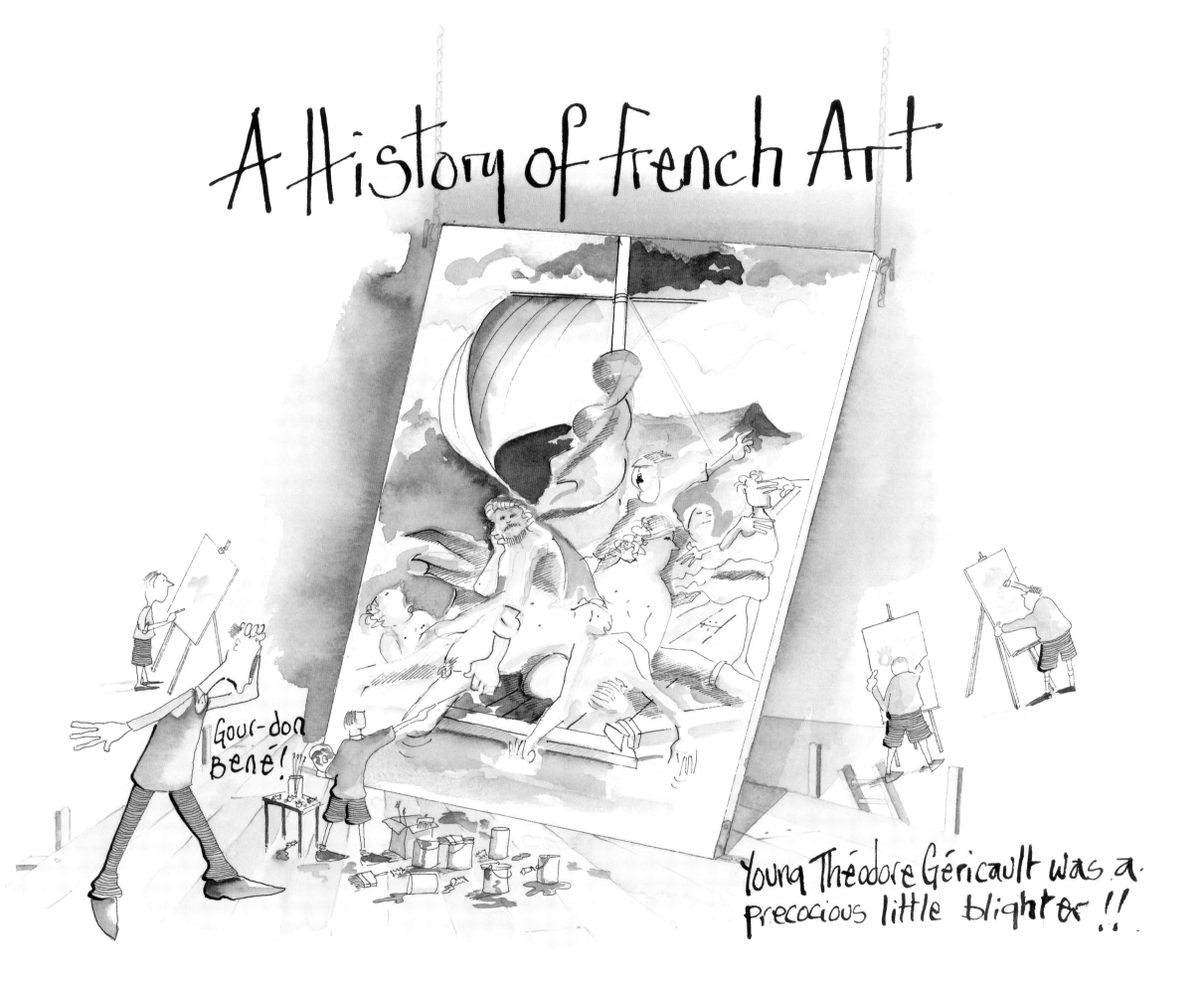

Édouard Manet 1832-1883

Manet championed the classics so it is ironic that he was always being attacked for his modernity. If you think Dejeuner sur L'Herbe caused a stink you should read what they said about his olympia (after analysing every cm of the exposed flesh of course!)

Claude Monet 1840-1926

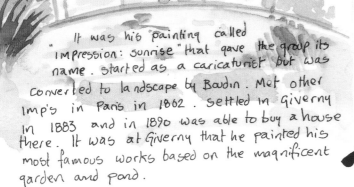

It was his painting called "Impression: sunrise" that gave the group its name. Started as a caricaturist but was converted to landscape by Boudin. Met other Imp's in Paris in 1862. Settled in Giverny in 1883 and in 1890 was able to buy a house there. It was at Giverny that he painted his most famous works based on the magnificent garden and pond.

Edgar DEGAS 1834-1917

the Impressionist Manet. Best his Contemporary as the ballet, and cafés. He best known for only bronze.

Introduced to circle by known for subjects such theatre, circus is probably his one and

The little Dancer Aged Fourteen 1880-1

Paul Cézanne 1839-1906

Greatest of the Post Impressionists. Family wealth sustained him which was just as well as he didn't receive his long overdue recognition until his last decade. Stuck to landscapes from 1870.

Pierre-Auguste Renoir 1841-1919

oi! keep yer 'ands to yerself yer dirty old sod!

Began work as a painter in a porcelain factory. lived in abject Poverty until 1881 when Durrand Ruel started to buy his work. The most accessible of the impressionists. "why shouldn't Art be pretty? He adored the female form. "I never think I have finished a nude until I think I could pinch it!" His son 'Jean Renoir (1894-1979) was the celebrated french film director.

Auguste RODIN 1840-1917

One of the great sculptors of history + the first to become a truly household name since Michelangelo. Rejected by the École des Beaux Arts three times. He was accused of cheating on another occasion because the sculpted anatomy was perfect. He gained fame in 1880 but controversy always followed him with commissioning committees unable to understand the subtleties of his genius.

I can't quite make out where the rock ends + the sculpture begins!!

Henri ROUSSEAU 1844-1910

Nicknamed Le Douanier (customs officer) because of his previous life in the Paris customs office (1871-93). Something of a fantasist, claimed to have served in Mexico with French Army and was unable to distinguish sarcasm from praise. Became full time painter in 1893 but achieved little success. Only after his death did his work gain recognition and influence with his bold shapes and bold colours. Tragically buried in a pauper's grave.

Georges Seurat 1859-1891

Founder of Neo impressionism. Well off parents so never worried about survival! He experimented by placing small touches of

unmixed colour side by side rather than mixing on the palette. The colours then merge when observed from a distance. The term Pointilism was thus coined to describe the technique. His most famous painting was titled 'Sunday Afternoon on the Island of La Grande Jatte'.
He died prematurely aged only 31. Officially he died of Meningitis but those who knew him said it was from over work.

Paul Gauguin 1848-1903

That doesn't look a bit like me!

Born in Paris but grew up in Lima. Back in Paris he became a successful stockbroker. In 1883 he became a full time artist. In 1886 abandoned wife + children + set up with fellow artists in Brittany. Then disastrously with van Gogh in Arles. In 1891 he leaves for Tahiti and despite abject poverty + disease paints his gloriously rich paintings depicting the natives.
Dies unknown, poverty stricken + riddled with syphilis. However his story is now the stuff of legend + he lives on in literature and film.

Henri de Toulouse-Lautrec 1864-1901

O.K. He was small due to two bad falls as a child, but he wasn't the ridiculous midget as is so often portrayed. In 1885 his eccentric nobleman father gave him an allowance to set up a studio in Montmartre and from 1888 began to portray aspects of theatre, Music Hall and Café life. His posters sealed his fame but like so many artists before + since he died of alcoholism + syphilis (very nasty indeed!)

Raoul Dufy
1877 - 1953

Painter, Graphic artist + textile designer. Started in an impressionistic style and converted to Fauvism in 1905. Well established by the 1920's + his bright, joyful technique helped to popularise modern art.

Marc Chagall
1887 - 1985

although born a Russian he is seen very much as a French artist. Despite long projects back in the Soviet Union he always returned + eventually settled in St Paul de Vence near Nice. His influences being taken mainly by either memories of a Russian Jewish childhood or the Bible. He always appeared to be other worldly and this inspired several ecclesiastical commissions.

Henri Matisse
1869   1954

THE SNAIL 1953

COLOUR IN HARMONY

Along with Picasso regarded as the foremost painter of his time. Started in a very traditional vein then on a trip to Brittany in 1896 he adopted a more impressionistic tone. He experimented with strong, bright colours and after a ground breaking exhibition at the Salon d'Automne he gave rise to the Fauve movement. From 1917 he lived on the Riviera.

Marcel Duchamp
1887 - 1968

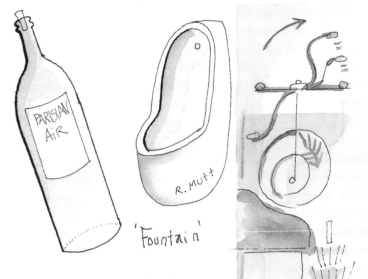

PARISIAN AIR

R. Mutt

'Fountain'

As much a man of ideas and influence as an artist producing finished work. Became a leader **coffee Mill** of the New York Dada movement. In 1912 invented the Ready Made, a bicycle wheel mounted on a kitchen stool. He caused an outcry by defacing the Mona Lisa (a copy!) He considered life meaningless + absurd + repudiated all the values of Art. Funny to think he is now seen as one of the greatest Artists of the Twentieth Century!

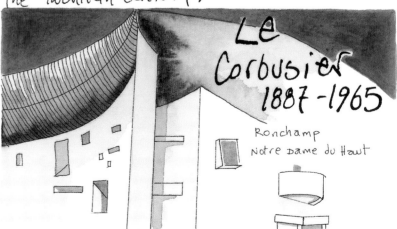

Le Corbusier
1887 - 1965

Ronchamp
Notre Dame du Haut

Chapter Eight

· · · · · · · ·

~ RACQUE ~

J'ai rendez-vous avec Mme Fru-Fru

Racque around the clock ~ A short Guide

LEGEND

1 Château Guillène (apartments)
2 Ruined Abbey
3 Church
4 Patisserie
5 Hairdresser
6 The Roman Bridge
7 The Town Hall
8 Bar Albert
9 Madame Fru-Fru's
10 Château Priaque (country club)
11 Bakers
12 Mini Super Market (8 till late!)
13 Florist
14 Gendarmerie (Wednesdays only)

A Souvenir from Racque

Early Beginnings!

The Romans hunted wild boar in the woods that ran along the valley of the Setrie and they built the first bridge around which Racque would eventually establish itself as one of the least known villages in rural France.

The Visigoths enjoyed the loose women and the wine and one can still recognise the Visigothian characteristics in many a Racque local on a Saturday night in the Bar Albert

Early Christian missionaries were soon seen off by the boorish and uncultivated inhabitants of this flea infested back-water. However they persisted and seventy five years later Reefus the Wily converted in a bid to introduce the Christmas Bank holiday to the area.

later attempts at conversion would include extracting finger nails, pouring hot oil down the pants and threatening close family members!!

While Empires rise and great cultures implode into oblivion Racque has remained blissfully unaware to these cataclysmic events, only when young men failed to return from Crusades, wars and hunting trips did people have an inkling of there being a world out side the valley of the Setrie.

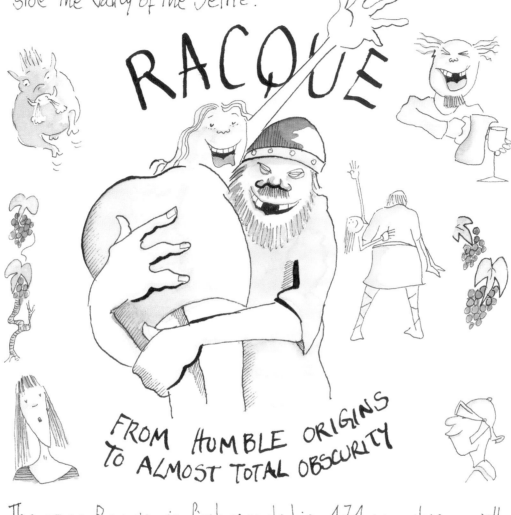

RACQUE

FROM HUMBLE ORIGINS TO ALMOST TOTAL OBSCURITY

The name Racque is first recorded in 474 A.D. when a well known inbred miscreant from Flabard called Bazille the Bludgeoner came over the hill to wreak havoc in the settlement with no name. Before conducting any number of a multiplicity of foul deeds Baz (as he was known by one and all) would clear his throat "Rracque!" and rather unnecessarily but totally within character would then spit on the ground whilst rubbing his great calloused hands together.

The first 'R' was dropped in 1209 when Peter the Pert went off to join the Albigensian Crusade. He didn't actually know what it was so he came home again but the first 'R' was now gone for ever!

BAZILLE THE BLUDGEONER

All good things must come to an end and Baz's end came soon enough when he was cornered by aggrieved locals and hacked to pieces just behind what is now Jeanne's the hairdressers at the bottom end of the Rue Columbine. His limbs and gizzards were then strung up a tree and fed to the ravens.

The Great DYNASTY

One family soon out did all the others for double dealing, cheating, lying and crawling in all the right places and in 1376 the humble Pierre Juste became the first Duc de Priaque. His son who was no less sycophantic and manipulative than his father had the title Duc de Guillène bestowed on him .... to be continued

The Dynasty ... continued

and the vast estate was therefore split in two with a hair raising complicated legal settlement that didn't prove that beneficial to anybody bar the money grabbing lawyers who concocted the document and prayed for calamity so they could come to the rescue and heap yet more gold into their coffers! Amazingly enough this eccentric set up worked well for almost two hundred years until 1547 when neither estate could produce a direct male heir.

The two conjoined estates then fell into the hands of two cousins, Patrice the Pitiful and Michael the Mildly Musical. It was this schism that ironically enough saw the first real rise in fortune for Racque which had up until then been a mere dung distribution centre for the surrounding vineyards.

Phooo-ee!

COME 'N GET YER luvly DUNG!

DUNG 1 GROAT a bucket

The Dynasty becomes a tyranny

The cousins in their small mindedness refused to allow any contact between the two estates whatsoever unless a toll was paid in order to gain access. Failure to prove payment (a brandmark on the forearm) would result in summary execution. However, in an effort to avoid paying the exhorbitant tarrif demanded by the greedy landowners goods and messages would be exchanged in secret at the settlement of Racque

by the Roman bridge.
Before long the enterprising peasants grew bold and were convinced that the levy had been repealed without proclomation. A large village comprising of several hundred fare dodgers began to appear in what had become a little state within a state.

Heh! Heh! Heh!

ooh look I've just found your husband!

Patrice and Michael though petty by nature were pretty ineffectual when it came to laying down the law. Michael's son Frank the Fanatically Ambitious however was a totally different kettle of fish! It was his intention to see the rule of law upheld in the most cruel manner imaginable. Thus it was on January 15th 1577 that a bunch of ugly bastards with Frank at their head rode into the centre of Racque and cut down every man, woman, child and living creature. This is still a black day in the history of Racque and on every January 15th the shops shut early and the Bar Albert sells half price drinks during a misery hour.

DOUBLE COGNAC

THIS BLASTED TRADITION COSTS ME A FLIPPING FORTUNE!

CHAMPAGNE!

a mega beer and a whisky chaser!

It's only a misery hour

For Albert Jean the present incumbent at the Bar Albert!!

The Monastery

Along side the Priaque~Guillène dynasty there co-existed in relative harmony the monks of the venerable order of Saint Belloysius (pronounced Bell-ees-er) who spoke only when spoken to by another monk but since a monk couldn't initiate conversation nobody ever spoke at all! The only words uttered in five hundred years of immaculate and sublime silence were "OW! BOLLOCKS THAT'S MY FOOT YOU CLUMSY BUGGER!" Translated from the Latin by Brother Thomas (in writing of course!) The breaker of the Holy seal of silence was Brother Simon for whom this was the last straw. On June 14th 1636 he was duly dismissed on one account of misappropriated funds, three accounts of drunkenness and an unspecified amount of accounts for leering and lewd behaviour especially with reference to displaying his nether regions to a visiting Abbot!

Poor Brother Simon disappears off into the Sunset!

The Glorious Revolution!

The French Revolution brought the greatest change with the Abbey Vineyards being seized by the revolutionary authorities and redistributed in an even handed and totally fair manner to the people.

Well not quite! The erstwhile Duc de Priaque~Guillène had renamed himself Thierry Toffkiller Hero of the masses Router out of the decadent, corrupt, degenerate and depraved Aristocracy. In his capacity as the Overseer of Rigorous Justice on the Supreme Council of Glorious Deputies of the Sons and Daughters of the Revolution (PHEW!) he thought it prudent to have the vineyards put under his temporary guardianship (AHEM!!) BY 1815 They were all his to keep!

THIERRY TOFFKILLER

The Eminence of Emile

Racque prospered throughout the 19th century as a mainly agricultural centre and market town. It was during this era of exploration and discovery that Racque produced its greatest son Emile Panachet (1833-1901) only child of Fabrice Panachet the local baker and his wife Claire. Emile was self taught and could speak the local dialect and count up to ten.

Bomb proof screen (his creation)

EMILE working on the exploding Beetroot Project for the French Army. He lost two fingers and, sadly, the contract.

He found not inconsiderable fame as an inventor and these few examples of his work will surely give rise to a nod of recognition

Panachet's Million+ soothing unction for Treatment + guaranteed ONE the cure OF EVERY DISEASE known to Man!

PANACHET'S UNCTION

PANACHET'S PATENTED HOT PANTS THAT KEEP PRIVATES PIPING ON PARKY PEREGRINATIONS!

Panachet's ingenious drinking vessel bolder and imbiber that keeps those hands busy whilst Quenching that thirst

Emile's Special Award

In 1873 Emile receives the prestigious Young Inventor of the Year Award. The more observant of you would have noticed that that makes him forty, so how could he qualify for such an award in the first place? His handwriting was such that the judges took him to be a minor! STILL, AN AWARD'S AN AWARD!!

He lived until his 68th year when he was last seen disappearing over the horizon in a prototype of his latest invention (see illustration) 'The Utterly Magnificent, Panachet's Flying Suit'. Somebody forgot to mention the fact that it was the opening day of the shooting season!

The Utterly Magnificent Panachet's flying Suit [PATENT PENDING]

LIFT OFF IN STYLE FROM YOUR BACK GARDEN AND ARRIVE AT YOUR MEETING FRESH, ENLIVENED. AND DRESSED FOR BUSINESS. (No callers Saturdays)

A Hero/Heroine for Today!

Another famous son of Racque had always been assumed to be a famous daughter until some unearthed paperwork discovered the true identity only last year.

LOUISE LAMARRE (1947-)

Just keep walking sweet pea!

MUM! MUM! she's got A moustache + she's smoking A PIPE!

Louise Lamarre the famous writer of Ladies' fiction is actually none other than Gérard Leboeuf son of Hubert the local cess pit pumper, part time vigneron and frequenter of the Bar Albert. Gérard left Racque shortly after his domineering father discovered his collection of Balenciaga scarves and a lingerie catalogue which concealed a receipt for two black camisole tops (large), six packs of seamed stockings and an industrial sized tin of depilatory cream.
Poor Gérard packed his bags for Paris that same evening. He soon became Poverty stricken and his straits rapidly encountered the dire!

what the B@X$! f!!÷∝ *e÷✗✗ !!!

From the Ashes!

Within a year of Gérard leaving Racque articles and short stories began to appear under the name of Louise Lamarre in the fiction sections of magazines such as 'Slic et chic', 'Go Go Girl' and 'Fab Femme'.
He (or is it she?) began to take heart from this moderate success and started in earnest on the first of many books.
In 1971 'The Misunderstood' was published to great acclaim closely followed by 'The Heavy Handed Heart' (Nov '71) 'Cruel + Heartless' and 'Down right Depraved!' (April '72) 'A father's wicked Ways' (December '72) 'Within an inch of Ecstasy' (May '73) and her most notorious book of all 'Tainted Juice a story from the Plantation' (November '73)

BIFF! grrr! OOF! HEL! CRUNCH!

The pressure, as can only be imagined by the relentless turnover of books soon began to take its terrible toll and tragically Louise began a demonic spiral into the dark world of drug abuse and costume jewellery evenings. The press hounded her and after one violent encounter Louise became a sad recluse.

Happily now Louise Lamarre is a grandmother living with a Bank Manager in Lyons and those heady days of Champagne receptions, book launches, promotional tours and physical abuse are long behind her. That doesn't mean to say that she has stopped writing, oh no, far from it! After a gap of nearly thirty years comes what will surely be her greatest success to date "From Maid to Madame ~ A young girl's rise from the Piggery floor to the Pigalle". Could this be at all autobiographical we ask ourselves? As a tribute to that literary genius and most loved old Racquienne we have been graciously granted permission to reproduce the opening lines from what will undoubtedly be words held on the lips of millions of adoring fans all over the World. This extract has been translated from the original French by Deryck killjoy.

Simone, her feet tired and sore, heaved her bosom before continuing the long and exhausting climb up the Mont du Droyard to the place of her new employ at the Château Vayenne. The rain a once fine gossamer mist is now a fearsome torrent and her bosom quivers 'neath her thin cape that barely covers her ample chest. Oh why hadn't she laid out something more substantial to wear that fateful morning? At last the forbidding gates, black and tumescent heave into view as a shattering crash of steely thunder rents the air like a cataclysm inflicted from the heavens by an avenging deity. Her bosom is now heaving like stink and the poor girl craves only the comfort of a friendly hearth.

As if in sympathy with her plight the once ferocious gods cease their clamour and the firmament parts as if in Eden the innocence of man is still intact. Her bosom heaves in glorious relief.

As she opens the massive gate a groan rises up from its tired hinges in sonorous welcome to the fresh faced stranger with the pert breasts. The gravel announces her arrival in strident crisp shots that can not be silenced however lightly she places her tiny, slender feet that are far from ample.

The great Bourbon pile rises before her, filling her pounding heart with dread and yet inexplicably a certain anticipatory excitement nestles in the inner reaches of her pure, unsullied soul.

"Is this to be the shape of things to come?" she ponders stroking the unusually shaped topiary that leads to the servants' quarters...........

From War to Peace

Modern times have seen Racque slip somnolently into a state of soothing solitude with an exodus of the young lured by the bright lights and excitements of the city and an influx (welcome if only for keeping the house prices bouyant) of foreigners from as far afield as Copenhagen and Crouch End. The last time Racque experienced 'visitors' was in 1944 when a Sherman Tank having split up from the liberating armies blundered into Jean Pondrelle's Patisserie demolishing 500 custard slices, 350 chocolate éclairs, 1600 Fairy Fancies and a wedding cake being iced for the following Saturday.

Warrl! Howdi Mayam!

Welcome Americaine Herrrros!

MY CAKES ARE RUINED YOU DAMN YANKEES!

The American crew namely Bill Erbhardt, Wally Schwarz and Dick Sullivan then left the tank after Mme Fru-Fru (the present Mme Fru-Fru's grandmother) made a patriotic gesture the boys just couldn't refuse.

As for the war itself really very little occurred outside of the mundane functions of a small farming community. A rather effete young German officer Baron Leutnant Karl Hapsbaum who loathed the Nazis

RACQUE TO-DAY

M. Rogue town clerk

WELCOME FRIENDS FROM BRITAIN

Village idiot

M. SANDRÉ - MAYOR

but adored English Romantic poetry and pressed wild flowers kept a cursory eye on the village while out collecting specimens and practising German Lieder for the camp concerts at the garrison in Ballerche. His Isolde was by all accounts quite stunning.

oh Fa La La La Fa La La!

The young German never lost his affection for the area and after several failed attempts to make a living on the stage he returned to Racque + married a local girl with whom he set up Happsi's Florist shop in the Rue Liberation. The natural animosity of the locals soon turned to intrusive meddling and finally he was made to feel welcome.

The Sun Never Sets on Racque

A Summer's evening in the new Millennium as the sun paints the surrounding hills in varying shades of gold and the gentle chime of goat bells brings the flock safely back into the fold. Racque remains comfortable in its role as a slumbering backwater managing somehow to survive with its idiosyncratic wine and rural charm.

The only ripple on an otherwise serene pond was when a certain Jacques.c.André made a successful bid for that most propitious of local appointments, the town mayor. He was just on the point of signing the contract that would secure a bottling plant and thirty five new jobs when a scandal involving Mme Fru-Fru (the grand-daughter!) three French loaves and a 4.5 litre tub of hand cleanser blew the entire shooting match out of the water. That was in 1977 and precious little has happened since BUT JUST SCRATCH THE SURFACE......

Citizens of Racque